THIS BOOK BELONGS TO

For Gwen and Perry

Warm thanks to B J Berti, Jasmine Faustino, and the dedicated staff at St. Martin's Press for their help and expertise; Paige Turner for her sharp eyes and clever wit; Julie Grant for her beautiful illustrations; all my friends, near and far, who encouraged me to make this book; and for all the children who discover the homemade way.

CREDITS: Pages 16, 17, 18, 20, 21, 22, 23, 24, 25, 26, 27, 28, 29, 30, 31, 34, 36, 38, 39, 40, 41, 43, 51, 54, 55, 56, 59, 61, 63, 70, 71, 72, 73, 74, 75, 95, 96, 98, 103, 104, 112, 113, 117, 122, 123, 125, 126, 127 © Julie C. Grant, Cover (Front), Page 3, © Blue Lantern Studio/Corbis, Page 14,16,17,18,19, Easy Steps in Sewing, for Big and Little Girls, or Mary Frances Among the Thimble People © 1916 The John C. Winston Company, Page 17 A Course of Study in Sewing Designed for Use in Schools by Olive C. Hapgood, ©1893, Page 20 Children's Literature, A Textbook of Sources for Teachers and Teacher-Training Classes (1920) by Charles Madison Curry and Erle Elsworth Clippinger, Pages 44-45, 64-65, 115 The Book House for Children ©1944, Pages 80-81,118-120, The Little Folks Handy Book Lina Beard and Adelia B. Beard, ©1910 Charles Scribner's Son, Page 136 E. Mackinstry ©1924 George H. Doran Company, Pages 134-135 Hand Shadows To Be Thrown Upon The Wall by Henry Bursill published by Griffith and Farran ©1859, Page 136 What Shall We Play? By E. Mackinstry, George H. Doran Company, ©1924.

Homemade Fun

101 Crafts and Activities to Do with Kids

Rae Grant

St. Martin's Griffin
New York

Also by Rae Grant:

Cooking Fun: 121 Simple Recipes to Make with Kids

Crafting Fun: 101 Things to Make and Do with Kids

www.stmartins.com

Written, designed, and produced by Rae Grant
Compilation copyright © 2010 by Rae Grant

Cover design Lisa Pompilio

The creators of this book have made every effort to emphasis safety precautions and safety procedures when children are cooking or baking in the kitchen and assume no responsibility for any child cooking without adult supervision. Any child in the kitchen should always be supervised by an adult.

Library of Congress Cataloging-in-Publication Data Available Upon Request

ISBN: 978-0-312-61077-7

First Edition: May 2010

10 9 8 7 6 5 4 3 2 1

A NOTE TO FAMILIES AND KIDS

Long ago, (yet still a recent memory for some), families celebrated the seasons and holidays, as well as the cycle of everyday life, in a homemade way. The homemade way sometimes appeared as a beautiful *Embroidered Pillowcase (page 37)* made by hand, or as *Paper Flowers (page 48)* made magically by someone who knew the ways of papercraft. The homemade way also appeared as *Sugar Cookie Cut-Outs (page 106)*, a *Sunshine Cake (page 100)* for a birthday, or a *Wooden Tool Box (page 112)* built by hand. Children in the family were given their own projects to make with an understanding that imagination would fill in where simplicity left off. Games were played, treats were baked, and toys were made at home. Children learned the rules of a game by playing it, they would understand how to fit boxes together to form a toy house by doing it. Birthdays were celebrated by making and decorating a cake and enjoying it together with friends and family at home.

People didn't realize that they had made a tradition out of homemade until it began to disappear. Treats and toys came from stores, playing invented games and making projects by hand were almost forgotten. Except by a few, who still remember....

Homemade Fun is a tribute to simple ideas for childhood fun. Many of the projects in this book are crafts that children have been making for generations. The directions and ideas are written to allow young crafters to try their hand at classic and imaginative projects with moderate adult supervision. I encourage you to keep the homemade tradition alive in your family and hope that some of the ideas in the book will inspire you to make and invent projects of your own too, at home. That's the homemade way! Enjoy making and doing at home.

Rae Grant
www.craftingfunforkids.com

TABLE OF CONTENTS

HAND SEWING AND EMBROIDERY 9
Recycled Containers 10
Sewing Equipment 11
Sewing Terms 12
Repurposing 13
Good Stuff to Repurpose 13
Rules for Hand Sewing 15
Threading a Needle 16
Making a Knot 16
Running Stitch 17
Backstitch 18
Creasing and Hemming 19
Buttons 20
Useful Embroidery Stiches 22
Up-and-Down Stitch 23
Straight Stitch Flower 24
Stem Stitch 25
Satin Stitch 26
Blanket Stitch 27
Crisscross Stitch 28
Chain Stitch 29
French Knot 30

Jelly Jar Lid Pin Cushion 31
Bluebird Ornament 32
Lunch Money Wallet 34
Embroidered Pillowcase 37
Placemat Roll-Up Pouch 38
Washcloth Puppet 40
Tooth Fairy Pillow 42
Soft Toy Bunny 44

PAPERCRAFTS 46
Paper Flowers 48
Paper Garland 49
Paper Lantern 50
Butterfly Wind Catchers 52
Beaded Cards 54
How to Address a Letter 55
Wall Art Calendar 56
Moon Journal 57
Simple Bookmarks 58
Folded Picture Book 60
Be an Author 61
Little Friendship Book 62
Critter Cutouts 64
Envelope Animals 65

MAKING JEWELRY 46

Salt Dough Beads 68
More Play with Salt Dough 69
Rolled Paper Beads 70
Button Bracelet 72
Bottle Cap Pin 74
Friendship Pin 75
Reversible Leaf Brooch 76
Leaf Art Journal 77
Acorn Jewelry 78
Owl Badge 79
Folded Paper Jewelry 80

BAKING 82

Baking Basics 84
Irish Soda Bread 86
Popovers 87
Busy Morning Biscuits 88
Cheese Pizza 90
Baked Pretzels 92
Olive Oil Bread 94
Double-Crust Pie Dough 95
Decorative Edging 96
Peach Pie 97
Pinwheels 98
Little Blueberry Tarts 99
Sunshine Cake 100
Mix-and-Match Frosting 102
Simple Decorations 103
Fancy Cupcakes 104

Sugar Cookie Cut-Outs 106
Colored Sugar 108
Cookie Icing Paint 109

BUILDING THINGS 111

Wooden Tool Box 112
Bottle Cap Name Plaque 114
Coffee Can Bird Feeder 116
Paper Sailboat 118
Cardboard Box Playhouse 122
Shoebox Dollhouse 124
Berry Box Doll Furniture 126
Clothespin People 127

TOYS, GAMES,
   AND PASTIMES 129

"Escargot" Hopscotch 130
Big Bubbles 131
Bubble Polo 131
Paper Cup Telephones 132
Silhouette Portrait 133
Shadow Pictures 134
Marbles 136
Clothespin Croquet 137
Jumping Rope 138
A Few Rules and
   Rhymes for Jumping Rope 139
The Ferret Runs,
   How He Runs 140
Musical Water Glasses 141

Hand Sewing
and
Embroidery

HAND SEWING AND EMBROIDERY

Recycled Containers

Sewing Equipment

Sewing Terms

Repurposing

Good Stuff to Repurpose

Rules for Hand Sewing

Threading a Needle

Making a Knot

Running Stitch

Backstitch

Creasing and Hemming

Buttons

Useful Embroidery Stitches

Up-and-Down Stitch

Straight Stitch Flower

Stem Stitch

Satin Stitch

Blanket Stitch

Crisscross Stitch

Chain Stitch

French Knot

Jelly Jar Lid Pin Cushion

Bluebird Ornament

Lunch Money Wallet

Embroidered Pillowcase

Placemat Roll-Up Pouch

Washcloth Puppet

Tooth Fairy Pillow

Soft Toy Bunny

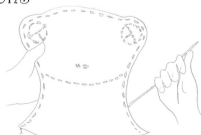

Recycled Containers

Everyday containers can be reused for storing your sewing supplies. Before you buy anything from the store, check in the cupboards and closets for useful throwaways. Look around your house for some of the containers listed below. Be sure to rinse and clean tins before using.

Berry boxes (wooden or cardboard)

Baking powder tins

Biscuit and cookie tins

Candy and gum tins

Cardboard cheese containers with lids

Cardboard oatmeal containers with lids

Drawstring bags

Lidded candy boxes

Plastic or metal toolbox

Shoeboxes with lids (adult or kid-size)

Small orange crates

Soap boxes

Straw baskets with lids

Tea tins and small tea boxes

Sewing Equipment

For the projects in this book, you will need the following supplies:

Buttons, eyelets, and snaps

Clear plastic ruler

Cloth tape measure

Craft scissors for cutting paper

Embroidery floss

Embroidery hoops (two 6-inch, either wooden or plastic)

Hand-sewing needles (size 6 or 7 sharps and large wide-eye needles)

Non-sharp metal or plastic blunted needle

Pencils with erasers for marking sewing lines

Pinking shears (optional)

Sewing basket or other recycled containers

Sharp scissors for cutting fabric

Small magnet for picking up stray pins

Straight pins (large, colored-head pins are easier to handle)

Safety pins

Thimble (metal or plastic)

Thread (good quality brand name in off-white or gray)

Water-soluble marking pens

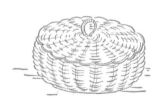

Sewing Terms

Fabric: Cloth or material woven from cotton, wool, linen, or silk. Soft cotton cloth (like muslin) is best for a beginner.

Selvage: The finished edge that runs lengthwise on a piece of fabric. It will not fray or unravel.

Raw edge: The edge of the fabric that is cut or torn.

Warp and weft: These are the threads of the cloth. The threads running lengthwise are the warp threads, and those running across from selvage to selvage are the weft. The warp is usually stronger than the weft.

Folded Edge: The edge made by doubling one part of the cloth over the other.

Wrong side: The side of the fabric that faces *in* when you wear a garment.

Right side: The side of the fabric that faces *out* when you wear a garment.

TIP *Wash and dry fabric before using to prevent shrinking.*

To tear a piece of cloth, make a 1-inch cut into the cloth. Holding the corner of each cut between the thumb and forefinger of each hand, pull the edges away from you and tear carefully.

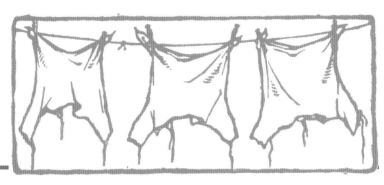

Repurposing

To repurpose an item is to take something old, like a shirt, and reuse it to make a new item. It's an old tradition and a good habit to practice when starting any craft project. Not only is it environmentally friendly to recycle as much as we can, it's also fun and challenging to create something new from a favorite old shirt or pair of pants. The very best place for you to look for material to repurpose is right in your own home, maybe even in your closet or dresser. It's a little like a treasure hunt—there's no telling what old and useful things you might find. Be sure to check with your parents before cutting anything.

Good Stuff to Repurpose

Aprons

Burlap

Baby blankets, cotton or fleece

Cotton clothing

Dish towels

Denim jeans

Felt scraps

Flannel pajamas

Fleece clothing

Flour sacks

Handkerchiefs or bandanas

Men's shirts with cuffs

Napkins or dish towels

Pillowcases or sheets

Placemats

Ribbon and string

Socks

Tablecloths

Washcloths or bath towels

To cut this pattern, fold goods twice, as indicated by dotted lines.

Pin patte... folded g...

Arrow ← pin this pattern ... of goods.
Two ring... that the ... must be placed on folded edges of goods.

PAT...

16...

USE THESE PAT...

14

All seams allowed.

Rules for Hand Sewing

1. Work with clean hands to avoid getting dirt or smudges on the fabric. Do not put any sewing material or equipment in your mouth!

2. Always sew with a thimble on the index or middle finger of the opposite hand holding the needle. Use it to push the eye-end of the needle through the fabric or to protect your finger when pushing the needle through fabric.

3. Avoid eye strain by working in a room with plenty of natural daylight or good lighting. It is best to sit in a sturdy chair with your sewing basket nearby.

4. When passing scissors or anything sharp to someone, be sure the tips are closed and the pointy side is facing down. This will prevent any accidental poking and pricks.

5. Protect your scissors by keeping them closed and stored in a small fabric case or a *Placemat Roll-Up Pouch (page 38)* when not in use.

TIP *Make a Jelly Jar Lid Pin Cushion (page 31) for storing pins and needles,*

Threading a Needle

A needle is a small piece of steel with a point on one end and a small opening on the other end. This opening is called the eye of the needle. Store your needles in Jelly Jar Lid Pin Cushion (page 31) or a needle case.

1. Measure and cut a length of thread about 12 inches. This length will help you manage the thread as you sew and prevent tangling and knots. Before threading your needle, snip off one end of your thread to make it even and smooth. This will allow you poke it through the eye of the needle more easily.

2. Next, hold the needle between the thumb and forefinger of your left hand, with the eye of the needle sitting a little above your pinched fingers. Moisten the tip of the thread to a point and then poke it through the eye of the needle. Pull the thread through about 3 inches and make a knot in the other end.

TIP *If you are having trouble threading your needle try holding the needle and thread above a white sheet of paper near a light.*

Making a Knot

To make a knot at the end of your thread, wrap the end around your index finger once or twice. Loosen the wrap a little bit and slip the loop off your finger. Slip the top end of the thread through the small loop and pull.

Running Stitch

This sturdy stitch is used to make a seam to hold two pieces of fabric together. The running stitch is made by running or weaving the needle in and out of the fabric using small, even stitches. (The stitches do not overlap.)

1. To practice a *Running Stitch*, draw a line on a piece of fabric. Thread your needle and tie a knot at the end. Poke the needle up through the back of the fabric until the knot tugs against the fabric.

2. Take a small stitch down and run your needle underneath the fabric along the line you have drawn.

3. Push the needle up from the other side just in front of the last stitch. Continue this method of going up and down in small stitches along your line.

4. When you come to the end, take the thread to the back of the fabric for the last stitch, but don't come up again. Secure the thread by weaving the end back through the stitching before clipping any extra thread.

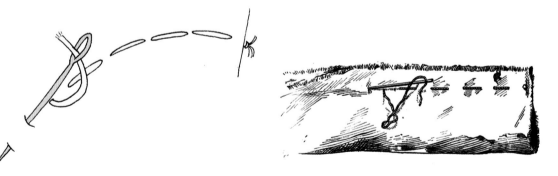

TIP *When using this stitch for an embroidery project, experiment with different thicknesses of thread to decide which you like best for your project. A thin thread will make a light line and a thicker thread make a wider or bolder one.*

Backstitch

Use a backstitch to make an extra strong seam. This stitch can also be used to make bold or delicate lines when embroidering.

1. Thread your needle and tie a knot at the end. Poke the needle up through the back of the fabric until the knot tugs against the fabric. Make one small stitch to the right of where your needle came up.

2. Next, weave the needle forward so it is in front of your starting point, about the length of a small stitch, and pull the needle all the way through (Figure 1).

3. Repeat as above. Go back towards your last stitch. Poke the needle down through the fabric, just in front of the last stitch. Pull the needle all the way through and begin the next stitch. Continue stitching the length of the line (Figure 2).

4. When you come to the end, take the thread to the back of the fabric for the last stitch, but don't come up again. Secure the thread by weaving the end back through the stitching before clipping any extra thread.

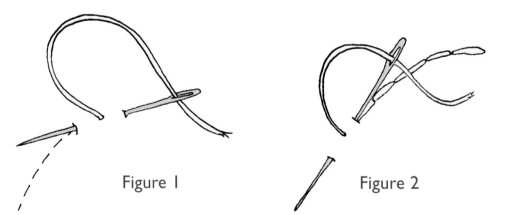

Figure 1   Figure 2

Creasing and Hemming

To hem is to turn fabric under in two small folds and sew the folded edge to the under layer. It is used for many of the sewing projects in this book.

1. A crease is made by folding the fabric and pressing along the edge with your thumbnail until a line is made. To prepare the hem, you will need to crease the fabric. First, fold the edge of the fabric down ½ inch and crease it well, then fold the fabric down another ½ inch and crease again.

2. Thread your needle and tie a knot at the end. Starting at one end of your project, poke the needle underneath the fold and pull it up through the folded edge until the knot tugs against the fabric (Figure 1). Tuck the knot under the edge using the point of the needle.

3. Point the needle into the fabric on a slant to take up two threads from the under layer and then through the fabric on the folded edge. Keep the needle on a slanted line pointing towards the left shoulder (Figure 2).

4. Continue making close and slanting stitches through all layers until you reach the end of the folded edge (Figure 3). When you come to the end, take the thread to the back of the fabric for the last stitch, but don't come up again. Secure the thread by weaving the end back through the stitching before clipping any extra thread.

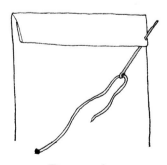

Figure 1

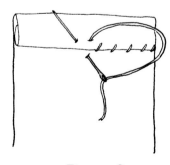

Figure 2

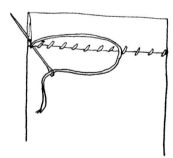

Figure 3

Buttons

At some point you will lose a button from your clothing and will want to repair it. Sew-through buttons are the most common type of button. They are flat with two or four holes. But buttons aren't only for practical things, they can also be used as decoration on fabric patches and small pillows.

1. Mark the place on the fabric where you want your button to go with a straight pin. (If you are mending you can usually find the old hole.)

2. Thread your needle and tie the end in a knot. Starting at **A** (Figure 1), pull the needle up through the back of the spot you have marked and place your button on the needle. Slide it to the end of the thread, against the fabric.

3. Next, poke the needle down through the second hole **B** (Figure 1) and into the fabric. Repeat the **A–B** step twice, and bring the needle back up through **C** and then down through **D** (Figure 2). Repeat the **C–D** steps twice. Finish with your needle under the button and tie the thread in a knot. Your stitches will have formed the letter "X" on the surface of the button.

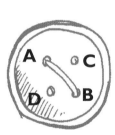

Figure 1

Figure 2

Figure 3

TIP *To sew on two-hole buttons first pull the needle up through the first button hole then weave the end back down through the second hole (see Button Bracelet page 72). Repeat threading through the hole twice and then finish as above.*

See a pin and pick it up,

All the day you'll have good luck;

See a pin and let it lay,

Bad luck you'll have all the day.

A Nursery Rhyme

Useful Embroidery Stitches

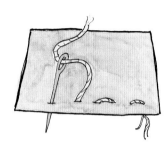

Up-and-Down Stitch

Straight Stitch Flower

Stem Stitch

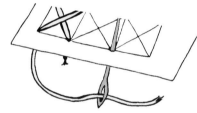

Crisscross Stitch

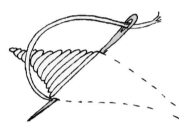

Satin Stitch

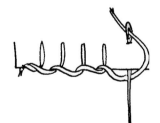

Blanket Stitch

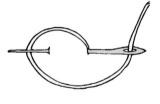

Chain Stitch

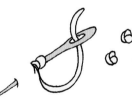

French Knot

Up-and-Down Stitch

The Up-and-Down Stitch (also know as a running straight stitch) is easy to learn and can be used to make simple creative designs. Use it to embroider a small decorative flower on fabric or sew two pieces of fabric together.

1. Thread your needle and tie a knot at the end. Poke the needle up through the back of the fabric until the knot tugs against the fabric (Figure 1).

2. Next, poke the needle down along the design or seam line (Figure 2). Pull the needle down through the fabric and then poke it up just in front of the last stitch. Continue going up and down along the line until you have reached the end of the fabric.

3. When you come to the end, take the thread to the back of the fabric for the last stitch, but don't come up again. Secure the thread by weaving the end back through the stitching before clipping any extra thread.

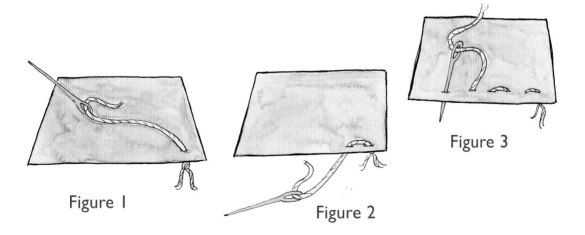

Figure 1

Figure 2

Figure 3

Straight Stitch Flower

Trace or draw a flower on your sample fabric to practice making flowers with the straight stitch.

1. Use a pencil to draw a flower on fabric (Figure 1).

2. Thread your needle and tie a knot at the end. At the outside end of one drawn line, poke the needle up through the back of the fabric and pull the needle through until the knot tugs against the fabric (Figure 1).

3. Next, position the needle at the inside end of the drawn line and poke down into the fabric. Weave your needle from underneath the end point, and come up at the beginning of the next inside line (Figure 2). Pull the thread lightly so that it lies flat on the line. (If it is a little twisted flatten it out with your fingers.) Take your needle to the back end point of the line and continue stitching until you finish.

4. When you come to the end, take the thread to the back of the fabric for the last stitch, but don't come up again. Secure the thread by weaving the end back through the stitching before clipping any extra thread.

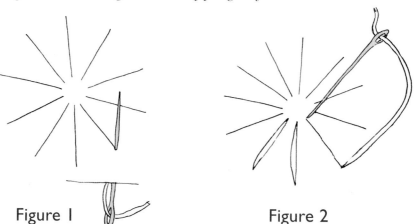

Figure 1   Figure 2

Stem Stitch

The stem stitch is good for outlining flower petals, curves, and stems.
The stitches are always sewn at a slant.

1. Thread your needle and tie the end in a knot. Poke the needle up through the back of the fabric and pull the thread through until the knot tugs against the fabric.

2. Make a *Straight Stitch (page 24)* from point **A** to **B**. Point the needle back towards point **A** and insert through the fabric at point **B**, then come through at point **C** (Figure 1). Pull the thread through gently.

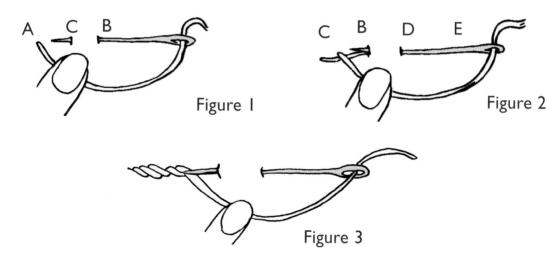

Figure 1

Figure 2

Figure 3

3. Next, take the needle back ¼ inch from your last stitch. Insert the needle through the fabric at point **D** and come back up through the fabric just right of the **B** hole (Figure 2). Repeat the same steps as described and continue stitching to the next point, keeping the tension even and the stitches the same length (Figure 3).

4. When you come to the end, take the thread to the back of the fabric for the last stitch, but don't come up again. Secure the thread by weaving the end back through the stitching before clipping any extra thread.

Satin Stitch

The Satin Stitch is used to fill in designs for leaves, stems, and flower petals. Use four to six strands of embroidery floss when working with this stitch. Be sure the fabric is tight in your embroidery hoop. This will help you make firm stitches.

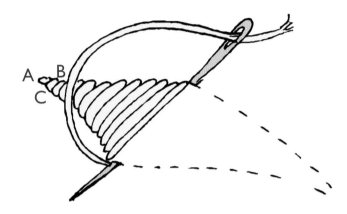

1. Draw a leaf shape design (*Leaf Art Journal, page 77*) onto your fabric.

2. Thread your needle and tie the end in a knot. Poke the needle up through the back of the fabric and pull the thread through until the knot tugs against the fabric.

3. Starting on the left side, come up at **A** and go down at **B**, making a *Straight Stitch (page 24)* the width of your leaf shape. Next, come up at **C**. Continue to sew the straight stitches close together across the leaf design. (You don't want to see the fabric peeking through between the stitches.) Work slowly and don't try to cover too large an area or the stitches will not fill in the shape tightly.

4. When you come to the end, take the thread to the back of the fabric for the last stitch, but don't come up again. Secure the thread by weaving the end back through the stitching before clipping any extra thread.

Blanket Stitch

The Blanket Stitch is used for finishing edges of fabric. You will start to see the stitch take shape after two or three stitches. If it doesn't look right, then start again or try to correct your practice stitch by reviewing the directions. This stitch is used for many of the projects in this book.

1. Thread your needle and tie the end in a knot. Poke the needle up through the back of the fabric and pull the thread through until the knot tugs against the fabric.

2. Next, poke the needle down through the fabric right next to the first stitch (Figure 1). Bring your needle up from underneath, making sure the point of the needle goes across the top of the loop. Pull gently to make the loop snug on the edge of the fabric (Figures 2).

3. Bring the needle back the same distance as your last stitch and push the needle down through the fabric and come up across the top of the loop. Continue on in even stitches until you reach the end (Figure 3).

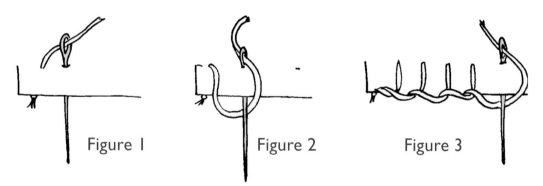

Figure 1   Figure 2   Figure 3

4. When you come to the end, take the thread to the back of the fabric for the last stitch, but don't come up again. Secure the thread by weaving the end back through the stitching before clipping any extra thread.

Crisscross Stitch

The Crisscross Stitch is made up of two straight stitches that form an X. You can make letters, borders and elaborate pictures using this basic stitch.

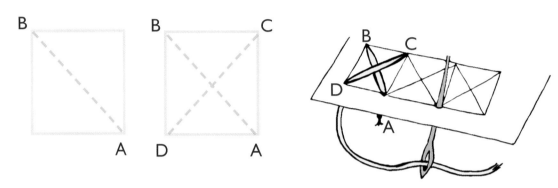

1. Thread your needle and tie the end in a knot.

2. Starting at the bottom right corner **A**, poke the needle up through the back of the fabric and pull the thread through until the knot tugs against the fabric.

3. Make a diagonal stitch to the upper left hand corner and insert your needle at **B**. Pull the thread through gently and then bring it up at **C**.

4. Make another diagonal stitch from **C** to the lower-left corner **D**. You will cross over the top of the first **A–B** stitch. Pull the thread through gently and continue making a row of stitches. When you come to the end, take the thread to the back of the fabric for the last stitch, but don't come up again. Secure the thread by weaving the end back through the stitching before clipping any extra thread.

TIP *To make a row of stitches, remember to always start in the lower-right corner of each square and end in the lower-left corner.*

Chain Stitch

The Chain Stitch makes a line of loops that resemble a tiny chain. Use it to outline a shape, border, or your name. Once you master making the first two loops the rest is really easy!

1. Thread your needle and tie the end in a knot. Poke the needle up through the back of the fabric and pull the thread through until the knot tugs against the fabric.

2. Hold the thread against the fabric with your thumb. Insert the needle back through the fabric next to the first stitch hole. Push the point of the needle down then weave back up. Your needle tip will cross over the top of the thread. Pull the thread gently to form the loop (Figure 1).

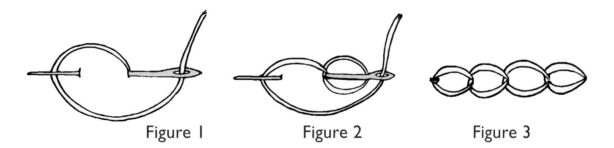

Figure 1   Figure 2   Figure 3

3. To make another loop, hold the thread with your thumb. Push the needle down through the fabric just inside the front of last loop and bring it back up. Pull the needle across the top of the thread to make the next loop (Figure 2). Continue to make loops in this way until you reach the end of your line (Figure 3).

4. When you come to the end, take the thread to the back of the fabric for the last stitch, but don't come up again. Secure the thread by weaving the end back through the stitching before clipping any extra thread.

French Knot

These little knots make perfect eyes for a Washcloth Puppet (page 40) or the center of a flower. They can also be used to make a pattern of polka dots. The number of wraps around the needle will determine the size of your knot. It may take several tries to get this right so be sure to practice this stitch.

1. Thread your needle and tie the end in a knot. Poke the needle up through the back of the fabric and pull the thread through until the knot tugs against the fabric.

2. Wind the thread around tip of the needle twice(Figure 1).

3. Hold the thread firmly against the needle with your left hand and poke the needle down through the fabric close to the same spot where you came up (Figure 2). Push the needle back into the fabric while holding the knot tightly in place under your thumb. (Be careful not to go through the same hole because the knot might slip through.) Bring your needle up through the fabric just to the left side of your last knot and continue (Figure 3).

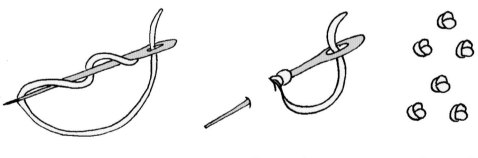

Figure 1   Figure 2   Figure 3

Jelly Jar Lid Pin Cushion

The lid and screw-on band from a canning jar can be transformed into a cute pin cushion.

MATERIALS NEEDED

Felt and fabric scraps

Lid and screw-on band (from a canning jar)

Jumbo cotton balls

Pencil

Scissors

White glue

Figure 2

Figure 3

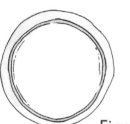

Figure 1

1. Lay fabric scrap, right side facing down, on the tabletop. Set the jar lid on top of the fabric and trace the circle. Remove lid. Draw another circle about 1 inch wider than the first circle onto the fabric and cut out (Figure 1). Next, trace the jar lid onto the felt and cut out the circle. Set aside for later use.

2. To make the pincushion mound, place the screw-on band, top side down, on the work surface. Next, set the fabric, right side down, into the band. Stack four to five jumbo cotton balls on top of the fabric to make a small fluffy "mound". Set the flat metal lid on top of the cotton balls and press firmly into the band (Figure 2). The fabric edges will push out from underneath the lid. Push the layers gently against the screw-on band until the lid is snug against the band and the mound pops through on the other side (Figure 3).

3. Dab glue on the inside edges of the fabric circle and press firmly, glue side down, until the fabric lies flat against the lid. To finish, dab glue onto one side of the felt circle. Set it inside the band, glued side down, on top of the fabric. Press well. Turn right side up and let dry.

Blue Bird Ornament

Make a classic bird-shaped ornament using the Blue Bird template (page 33) or draw your own picture and shape. Young children can use a shoelace to practice sewing their ornament.

MATERIALS NEEDED

Tracing paper or lightweight brown bag

Scissors

Tape

Lightweight cardboard (cereal boxes)
colorful card stock

Pencil

Hole punch

Large-eye needle

Embroidery floss, or yarn,
about 12 inches long

1. Assemble all materials on your work surface. Use a pencil to trace the bird-shaped template onto tracing paper. Cut out the shape to use as a pattern.

2. Tape the pattern to the cardboard or cardstock and trace the shape again. Remove the pattern from the cardboard or cardstock and set aside. Use scissors to cut out the shape. Make evenly spaced holes along the outside edge of your shape using the hole punch.

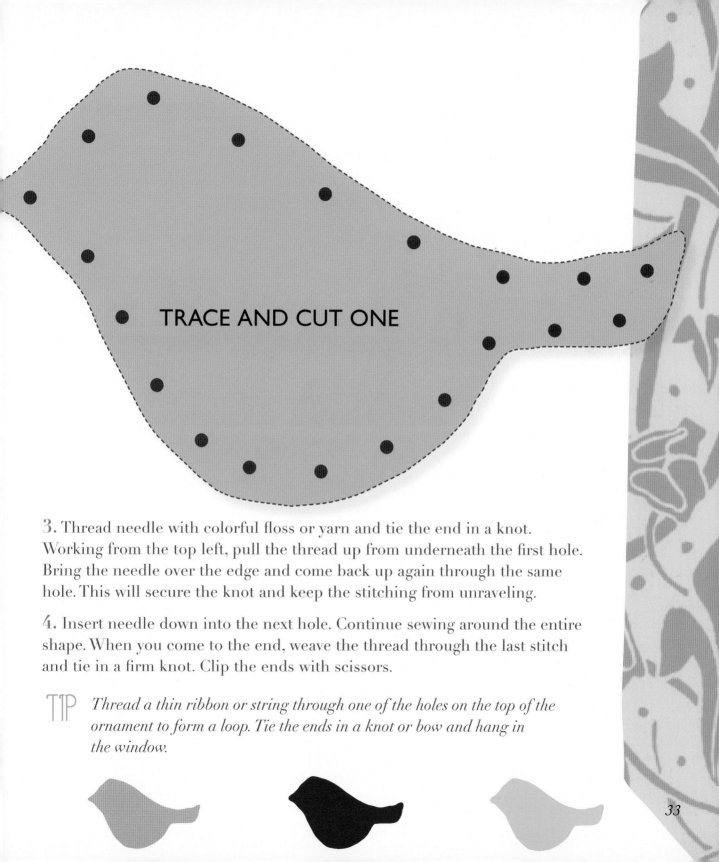

TRACE AND CUT ONE

3. Thread needle with colorful floss or yarn and tie the end in a knot. Working from the top left, pull the thread up from underneath the first hole. Bring the needle over the edge and come back up again through the same hole. This will secure the knot and keep the stitching from unraveling.

4. Insert needle down into the next hole. Continue sewing around the entire shape. When you come to the end, weave the thread through the last stitch and tie in a firm knot. Clip the ends with scissors.

TIP *Thread a thin ribbon or string through one of the holes on the top of the ornament to form a loop. Tie the ends in a knot or bow and hang in the window.*

Lunch Money Wallet

Make a wallet to store your lunch money and library card.

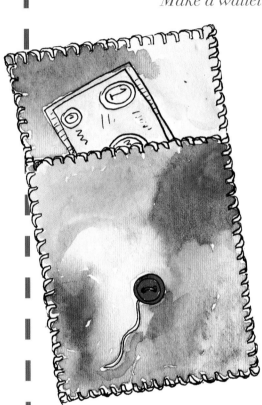

MATERIALS NEEDED

Pencil

Ruler

Tracing paper

Pins

Scissors

8-by-3¼-inch felt or fleece

Large-eye needle

Embroidery floss,
about 18 inches long

Two buttons

Thin ribbon or string, about 4 inches long

1. Assemble all materials on your work surface. Use a pencil and ruler to trace the template on tracing paper (Figure 1). Pin pattern to felt and cut out the shape.

2. Use ruler to measure 6½ inches up from the bottom on both edges of the rectangle. Mark each point with your pencil. Use ruler and pencil to connect the two points.

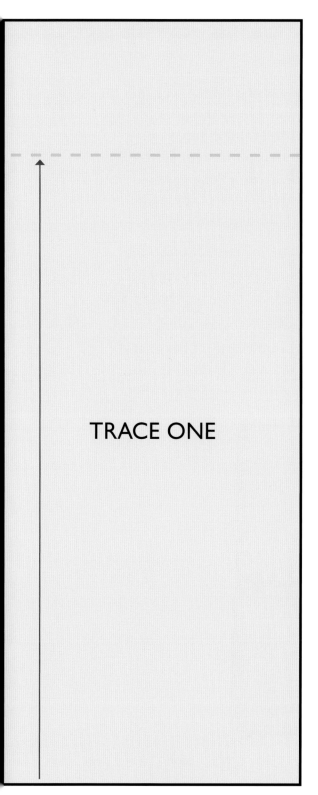

TRACE ONE

Figure 1

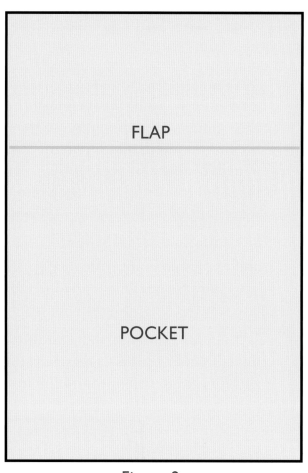

FLAP

POCKET

Figure 2

3. Fold the bottom edge up to the pencil line and crease well along the bottom to make a fold (Figure 2). Pin sides together to form a pocket. Thread your needle and tie the end in a knot. Make a *Blanket Stitch (page 27)* around the sides and top flap, sewing all the way around the wallet. When you come to the end, take the thread to the back of the fabric for the last stitch, but don't come up again. Secure the thread by weaving the end back through the stitching. Clip extra thread. Remove pins.

4. Next, *Blanket Stitch* along the top edge of the pocket (be careful not to stitch the pocket shut!). Secure the thread as above.

5. To make a flap, fold down the top single layer of the fabric over the pocket crease well. (The flap will overlap the top edge of the pocket.) Next, find your center point on the top edge of the folded flap. Center the button top to bottom on the flap and mark that point with your pencil. Unfold and turn fabric over (pocket side down). Poke your threaded needle up from the bottom, through the center of the mark. Place button on the needle and sew on firmly. Fold flap down again.

6. Center the second button on the pocket about 1 inch below the flap and mark that point with your pencil. The buttons should be lined up. This time, bring the threaded needle up through the *inside* of the pocket and sew the second button on firmly (*Buttons, page 20*).

7. To make a tie, wrap one end of the string around the top button and tie in a knot to secure. Crisscross the string around the bottom button and then wrap twice around the top button to close and secure wallet.

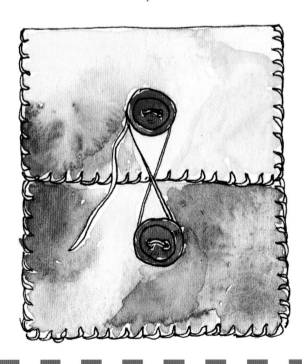

Embroidered Pillowcase

Make a sampler pillowcase using a variety of Useful Embroidery Stitches,
(page 22). The Straight Stitch Flower (page 24), and the Blue Bird (page 32)
are all good beginning embroidery drawings to trace and stitch.

MATERIALS NEEDED

Pencil

One sheet of tracing paper

Soft lead pencil

White cotton pillowcase

Needle

Embroidery floss (assorted colors)

1. Use a pencil to trace or draw a simple design onto the tracing paper. To transfer a design, set the illustrated side of the paper face down on a hard surface. Using a soft lead pencil, rub over the back of the drawing until it is completely covered with a layer of pencil marks.

2. Next, determine where to place your design on the fabric. Set the tracing paper, pencil-rubbed side facing down, in position. Use a pencil to retrace the design onto the fabric. Press down lightly as you trace. (The pressure from the pencil will transfer the image onto the fabric.) When finished, remove paper. Check that the traced pattern has been transferred to the pillowcase.

3. Choose from *Useful Embroidery Stitches* (page 22) to embroider your drawing as you wish. When you have finished stitching, wash fabric in cold soapy water to remove any smudges from the tracing paper or pencil. Pat dry in a towel and hang to dry.

Placemat Roll-Up Pouch

A repurposed placemat makes a handy roll-up pouch in no time at all. Use to store art supplies, a small notebook, pencils and paints, maps, or even small dolls and little treasures.

MATERIALS NEEDED

14-by-19-inch fabric placemat (medium weight)

Pins

Large-eye needle

Heavy thread

Pencil

Scissors

1-inch wide ribbon, about 24 inches long

1. Assemble all materials on your work surface. Set placemat in front of you lengthwise. The right side of the fabric will be facing down.

2. To make a pouch, bring the bottom edge of the placemat up about ¾ of the length of the rectangle (Figure 1). Crease the bottom fold and pin each side together. *Back Stitch (page 18)*, the edges together in small, tight stitches. Remove pins when done. You will have a sewn one long pouch with an opening (Figure 2).

3. To make four smaller pockets, fold the bag in half and crease the outside edge firmly. Fold in half again and crease the outer edge firmly, then unfold the entire placemat. You will have four equal creases across the placemat (Figure 3). Use pencil to draw a light line along each crease.

4. Starting at the bottom, sew along each crease line using the *Running Stitch* (*page 17*). Make small steady stitches until you reach the top of the pocket. When you come to the end, take the thread to the back of the fabric for the last stitch, but don't come up again. Secure the thread by weaving the end back through the stitching before clipping any extra thread. (You will have four pockets.)

5. To make ribbon tie: Fold the ribbon in half. Pin the folded end of the ribbon onto one side edge of the placemat. Place it halfway up from the bottom (Figure 4). Use the running stitch to secure the ribbon to the mat. Starting with the side without the ribbon, fold or roll-up the pouch. Wrap the ends of the ribbon around and tie both ends in a bow. Your roll-up pouch is ready to use!

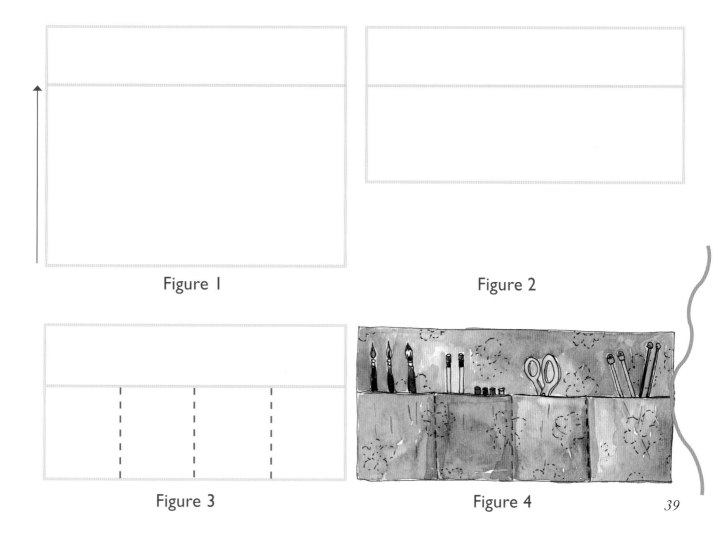

Figure 1

Figure 2

Figure 3

Figure 4

Washcloth Puppet

Use two clean washcloths to make a puppet for the bathtub. Trace the frog face template or draw your own simple face.

MATERIALS NEEDED

Pencil

Tracing paper or lightweight brown bag

Two washcloths

Pins

Scissors

Embroidery hoop

Large-eye needle

Embroidery floss or heavy thread

1. Assemble all materials on your work surface. Use a pencil to trace the pattern onto tracing paper.

2. Place washcloths together and carefully pin the pattern to the top of the fabric. Use scissors to cut out two identical shapes. Remove pins and tracing paper. Set one washcloth aside.

3. Use a pencil to draw or trace the frog face *(page 41)* onto one washcloth. Set washcloth firmly in an embroidery hoop and secure. Thread your needle with floss and tie the end in a knot. Use the *Running Stitch (page 17)*, to outline the face and mouth. Embroider the eyes with the *Satin Stitch (page 26)*. Make the nose using *French Knot (page 30)*. When you have finished, remove washcloth from the embroidery hoop.

4. To assemble puppet: Pin the two washcloths together, with the embroidered side facing in. Use the *Running Stitch (page 17)* to sew the sides and top edges in firm, even stitches. Hem the bottom *(page 19)* along both bottom edges to prevent fraying. When you are finished, turn the fabric right side out and try on your hand puppet!

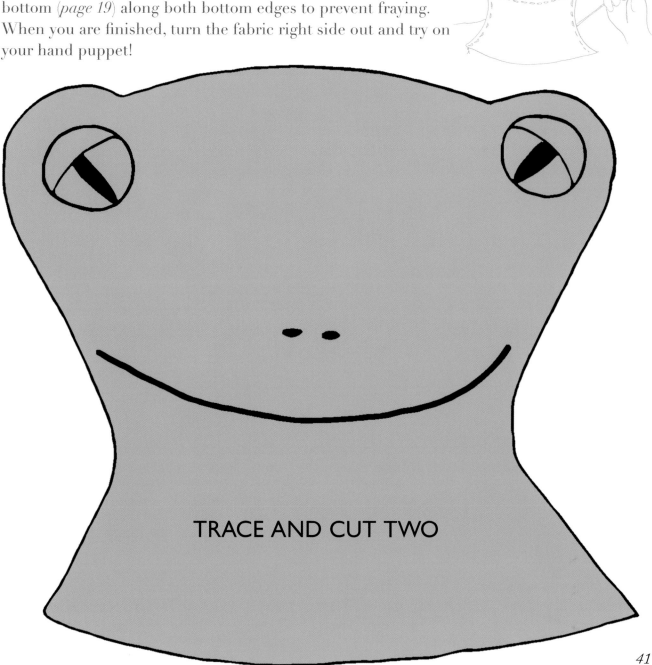

TRACE AND CUT TWO

Toothfairy Pillow

This little pillow is the perfect size for a lost tooth and a note to the tooth fairy.

MATERIALS NEEDED

Pencil

Ruler

Two pieces of 4-by-5-inch felt or heavy cotton (any color)

Scissors

One piece of 3-by-3-inch felt (any color)

Pins

Large-eye needle

Embroidery floss, about 12 inches long

A bag of jumbo cotton balls or cotton batting

1. Assemble all materials on your work surface. Use a pencil and ruler to draw 4-by-5-inch shapes on the larger piece of felt or fabric.

2. Use scissors to cut around the outlines to make two matching pieces. Set aside.

3. To make a tooth pocket: Measure and cut a 2-inch heart from the smaller piece of felt. Place the pocket heart in the center of the larger piece. Pin the heart in place.

4. Next, thread your needle and tie the end in a knot. Using the *Running Stitch (page 17)*, insert needle from the back and come up at the top left of the heart. Sew down along the left side of the heart in small even stitches, until you reach the top right side. (Be careful not to stitch the pocket shut!) When you come to the end, take the thread over for the last stitch and come up again. Weave the thread through the stitch and tie in a firm knot. Clip ends with scissors.

5. To make your pillow: Pin the front and back of the larger pieces together with the right sides facing out. Use the *Running Stitch (page 17)* to sew along the sides and bottom edge in small, even stitches. Leave a wide opening at the top for your stuffing.

6. Gently stuff the pillow by pushing the cotton balls in through the opening with a pencil. Once the pillow is tightly stuffed sew the top closed. When you come to the end, take the thread over for the last stitch and come up again. Weave the thread through the stitch and tie in a firm knot. Clip ends with scissors. Place tooth in heart pocket and hide it under your pillow before you go to sleep.

TIP *If you would like for your pillow to have a pleasant smell, dust a teaspoon of scented talcum powder over the cotton balls before stuffing.*

Soft Toy Bunny

This is the perfect beginner sewing project. Denim fabric from old jeans is a good fabric to use. It is soft, durable, and easy to stitch.

MATERIALS NEEDED

Pencil

Tracing paper or lightweight brown bag

Pins

Two pieces of 9-by-5-inch denim

Scissors

Large-eye needle

Embroidery floss or heavy yarn

Thin ribbon

A bag of jumbo cotton balls or cotton batting

1. Assemble all materials on your work surface. Use a pencil and tracing paper to outline the pattern of the bunny (Figure 1). Cut out the shape and pin the pattern onto both pieces of fabric. Use scissors to carefully cut around the shape.

2. With right sides facing out, pin the wrong side of fabric pieces together at the top, center, and bottom. Leave an opening for stuffing the pillow along one side.

3. Thread a needle with embroidery floss or heavy yarn. Using the *Blanket Stitch (page 27)*, sew the pieces together in even stitches (Figure 2). Gently pack small amounts of stuffing as you sew around the edges (Figure 3).

4. When the bunny is stuffed, stitch the opening shut. When you come to the end, take the thread over for the last stitch and come up again. Weave the thread through the stitch and tie in a firm knot. Clip ends with scissors. If you like, tie a colorful ribbon around the bunny's neck.

TRACE ONE

Figure 1

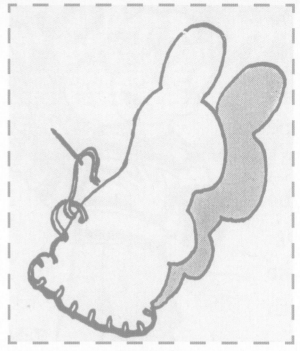

Figure 2

Figure 3

45

Papercrafts

Paper Flowers
Paper Garland
Paper Lantern
Butterfly Wind Catchers
Beaded Cards
How to Address a Letter
Wall Art Calendar
Moon Journal
Simple Bookmarks
Folded Picture Book
Be an Author
Little Friendship Book
Critter Cutouts
Envelope Animals

Paper Flowers

Use decorative tissue paper recycled from gift boxes to make colorful paper flowers. Use as decorations on presents, or pin onto hats and scarves. Try tripling the paper circles for a fuller flower.

MATERIALS NEEDED

Decorative tissue paper, assorted colors

Lid from a jar

Pencil

Scissors

1. Assemble all materials on your work surface. To make a double-layered flower, you will need two circles of tissue paper. Using a pencil, trace a circle onto two layers of tissue paper using the jar lid as your template.

2. Keep the cut circles together and fold in half (from left to right), then fold again from the top to bottom (Figure 1). Use scissors to cut along the outer edge to make a scalloped shape (Figure 2).

3. Open up the circle and gently pinch the center from underneath to form a flower. Twist the back to make a small stem. Adjust petals to open (Figure 3).

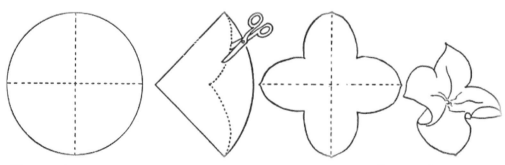

Figure 1   Figure 2   Figure 3

Paper Garland

Paper garlands are beautiful to hang along a window any time of year. Use assorted tissue paper to make an extra-colorful design.

MATERIALS NEEDED

Paper Flowers (page 48), about twelve

Thread, about 30 inches long

Large-eye needle

Clear tape

1. Follow instructions for making *Paper Flowers (page 48)*. Gather all your paper flowers and place on a tray. Measure a thread about 24 inches long. Thread your needle and tie the end in a knot, leaving a 6-inch tail on the end for hanging.

2. Poke your needle through the inside middle of the flower and pull the needle through until the knot tugs against the paper. Slide the flower to the base of your thread until it hits the knot. Continue threading the needle through the center of each flower as described above. Make more flowers and tie on additional thread to make the garland longer.

3. When you have sewn the last flower, tie the thread in a knot, leaving a 6-inch tail for hanging. (The knot will prevent the flowers from slipping off.) Tape the garland in a doorway, a window, or drape it across a mantle.

Paper Lantern

The Lantern Festival is an important celebration that takes place during the Chinese New Year. Make a lantern from red construction paper (in Chinese traditions, red symbolizes good luck).

MATERIALS NEEDED

8½-by-11-inch sheet of construction paper, for each lantern

Scissors

Clear tape

Strip of construction paper

White glue or clear tape

1. Assemble all materials on your work surface. Fold a sheet of paper in half from right to left (Figure 1). You should have a folded edge on the right side (Figure 2).

2. Starting about 1 inch up from the bottom, use scissors to cut across the folded edge, almost to the open edge. (Be careful not to cut all the way through.) Continue to cut evenly spaced lines until you are about 1 inch from the top.

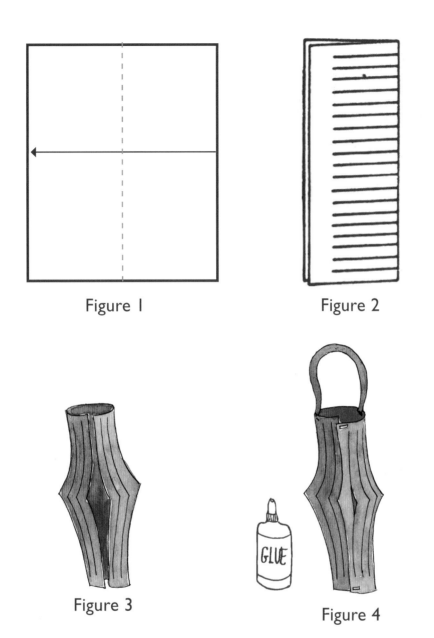

Figure 1

Figure 2

Figure 3

GLUE

Figure 4

3. Unfold and roll the paper so the edges overlap to make a tube shape (Figure 3). Tape the overlapped paper edges together. To make a handle for hanging, cut a strip of paper to the desired length and glue or tape each end to the top left and right sides of the lantern (Figure 4).

TIP *You can make smaller lanterns and vary the spacing between the cuts. String a dozen small lanterns on a long ribbon and use as party decorations for an outdoor picnic or a birthday party.*

Butterfly Wind Catchers

Wind catchers are a whimsical way to experiment with cut-and-fold decorative objects. Cut and decorate butterflies and sew onto long threads to hang from a twig or an embroidery hoop.

MATERIALS NEEDED

3-by-4-inch piece of newspaper
or construction paper, for each butterfly

Pencil

Scissors

Strips of colored paper

Markers and stickers

White glue

Large-eye needle

Thread

Thin twig or embroidery hoop

Twine or ribbon, about 18-inches long

1. Assemble all materials on your work surface. For each butterfly, fold a sheet of paper in half (Figure 1). Use a pencil to draw the shape of the butterfly wings (Figure 2).

2. With the paper folded, use scissors to cut out the butterfly. Open to view. (The folded edge will be in the center.) Decorate with markers, stickers, or try *Useful Embroidery Stitches (page 22)* to decorate the wings.

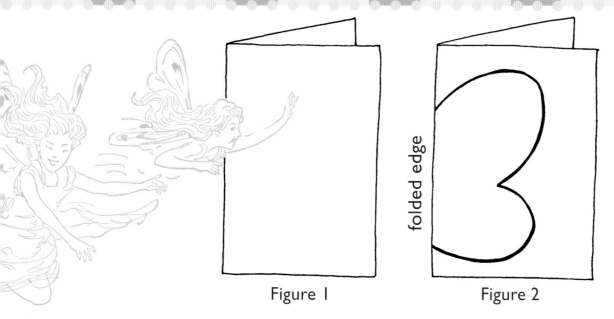

folded edge

Figure 1   Figure 2

3. **To make antennae:** Cut two thin strips of contrasting paper the length of the center fold. Wrap the end of one strip around a pencil to make a curl. Glue the strip to the center along the fold. Press well and let dry. Repeat with the second strip. Make as many as desired.

4. **To make a mobile:** Gather paper butterflies and place on a tray. For each butterfly measure a thread 12 inches long. Add an extra 6 inches on the end for hanging. Thread your needle and tie the end in a knot.

5. Next, poke your needle through the top of the middle fold of a butterfly and pull the needle up until the knot of thread tugs at the back of the paper. Set aside. Continue threading each butterfly as described above.

6. When finished, tie each in a simple knot around the twig or hoop making each a different length. Space each butterfly evenly across the branch or around the hoop. Tie a length of twine or ribbon around both ends of the twig or sides of the hoop to form a hanger. Place the hanger on a hook in a window to catch the breeze.

TIP   *Use newspaper and decorative tissue paper to make one large butterfly or a fluttering fish. Sew thread though the center fold and hang from a string in a breezy place.*

Beaded Cards

Beaded cards are always a special keepsake for friends and family.
Make several and start an exchange with other crafter friends.

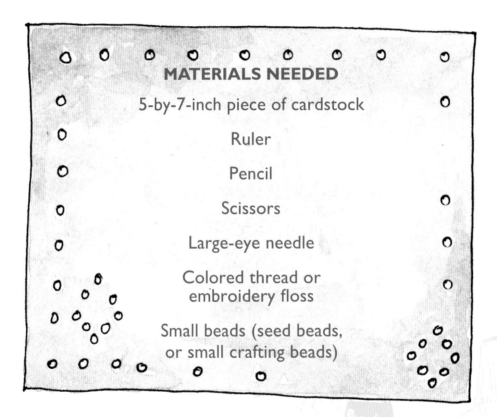

MATERIALS NEEDED

5-by-7-inch piece of cardstock

Ruler

Pencil

Scissors

Large-eye needle

Colored thread or
embroidery floss

Small beads (seed beads,
or small crafting beads)

1. Assemble all materials on your work surface. Use a pencil to draw a pattern of dots on the card as guides for stitching (see above). Set the card on a work surface and use a needle to poke a series of holes about ½ inch apart along the edges. (It's OK if the pattern is irregular.)

2. To begin beading, measure a 12-inch length of thread then double the length. Thread your needle and tie both ends together in a knot. (You may have to add more thread later.)

3. Working from underneath the card, poke the needle up through the first hole and gently pull the thread through until the knot tugs against the card.

4. With your needle on the front of the card, thread enough small beads to fill a ½ inch space and slide each one down the needle to the base of the thread. Weave the needle down into the next hole and back up through the next hole. Pull the thread gently to tighten so the beads will lay flat and even.

5. Continue to bead until you reach the last hole. When you come to the end, weave the thread through the last stitch and tie in a firm knot. Clip ends with scissors. Place in a proper-sized envelope to mail.

TIP *Experiment with the different stitches in the Useful Embroidery Stitches (page 22) section of this book to make a variety of stitched designs.*

How to Address a Letter

It is important to know how to write an address properly to make certain that your letter can be delivered to the correct person. Use a good pen or pencil and your best handwriting and follow the example below.

Your name

Street address

City, State, Zip Code

> Place Stamp Here

Name of recipient

Street address

City, State, Zip Code

Wall Art Calendar

Make a simple art calendar using a favorite painting or postcard .

MATERIALS NEEDED

Heavy cardstock

Pencil

Ruler

Scissors

White glue or glue stick

Favorite art or postcard

Hole punch

Ribbon or cord

Small paper calendar
(from stationery store)

Calendar

1. Assemble all materials on your work surface. Use a pencil and ruler to measure a 6-by-9-inch rectangle on cardstock. Use scissors to cut it out.

2. Choose a favorite picture or postcard to fit on the top half of your calendar (trim to size if necessary). Glue the back of the picture and place it, glued sided down, on the front of the cardstock. Press well. Next, glue the back of calendar and place it underneath the picture. Press well and let dry.

3. To make a hanger: Use a hole punch to make two holes at the top of the calendar (about 1 inch in from either side), and thread the ribbon through both holes. Knot the ribbon at both ends in the back.

Moon Journal

Did you know that we did not always have written calendars to help us keep track of days of the week? Some older societies, such as Native Americans, used the moon as a guide to track the time of year and season. Observe the moon throughout the course of a month and record findings in your *Moon Journal*. Be sure to invite your family to join in your moon gazing. Ask your librarian to recommend a book which explains all about the phases of the moon. Draw a moon chart in the moon journal.

Simple Bookmarks

Once you learn to make this bookmark, you will never again have to bend down the corners pages of your book to mark your place. Make a variety of animal-shaped bookmarks using this simple technique and give to friends and family.

MATERIALS NEEDED

Tracing paper

Brown or green cardstock or cereal box cardboard

Pencil

Scissors

Colored pencils

Paper scraps

White glue

1. Assemble all materials on your work surface. Use a pencil to trace the owl template onto tracing paper. To transfer the drawing, set the illustrated side of the paper face down onto a piece of cardstock or cardboard (Figure 1). Using a soft lead pencil, rub over the back of the drawing until it is completely covered with a layer of pencil marks.

2. Set the tracing paper, pencil-rubbed side facing down, in position. Use a pencil to retrace the design onto the cardstock. Press down lightly as you trace. (The pressure from the pencil will transfer the image onto the fabric.) When finished, remove paper. Check that the traced pattern has been transferred to the cardstock or cardboard. Use scissors to cut out the shape. You can also draw your own shape if you wish.

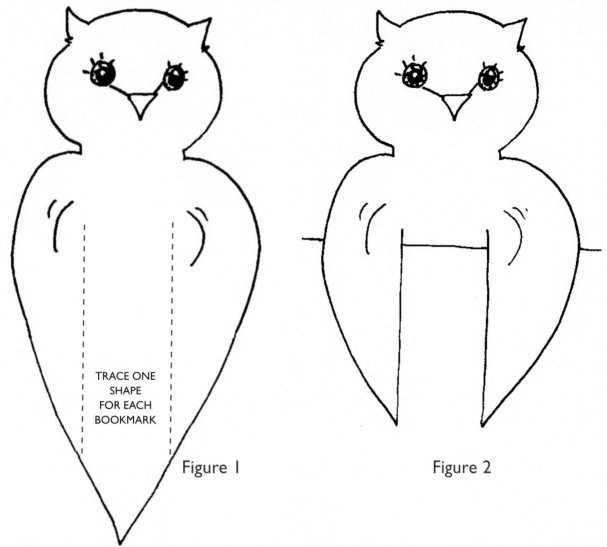

TRACE ONE
SHAPE
FOR EACH
BOOKMARK

Figure 1

Figure 2

3. Decorate the owl face and feet using colored pencils or paper scraps. Tear small bits of scrap paper to make feathers and colored details. Glue onto the owl as you like. Let dry.

4. To make a tab for the bookmark: Use scissors to cut along the dotted lines (Figure 1). The length of your cut should be the same on each side. Place the tab behind a book page and position the wings to overlap the page you are marking (Figure 2).

Folded Picture Book

Make a three-panel picture book using this simple method for folding and gluing pages together. Write a story about your life or about your family, or favorite pet. Add photographs or draw pictures to illustrate your story.

MATERIALS NEEDED

Three sheets of 8½-by-11-inch white cardstock

Old paintbrush

White glue

Heavy book (for pressing)

Paints, colored pencils, markers, rubber stamps

Hole punch

Two pieces of ribbon or string, each about 12 inches long

1. Assemble all materials on your work surface. Fold three sheets of 8½-by-11-inch card stock in half widthwise to make three 5½-by-8½-inch folded sheets. Crease well along each fold.

2. Open the first sheet and place on your work surface with the creased edge facing up (Figure 1). Apply glue to right panel (**A**) and set the second sheet (**B**), with crease facing down, on top. Align edges and press well. Your book should look like Figure 2.

3. Open the third sheet with the creased edge facing up (Figure 3). Apply glue to panel (**D**) and align edges with the back of (**C**). Press well.

4. Fold the book together (it will close like an accordion or fan) and set a heavy book on top. Let it dry. Decorate and illustrate the cover and pages however you like.

5. To make a tie for your book, make a hole punch on the outer left and right panel (Figure 4). Thread a ribbon or string through each hole and tie the ends in a bow.

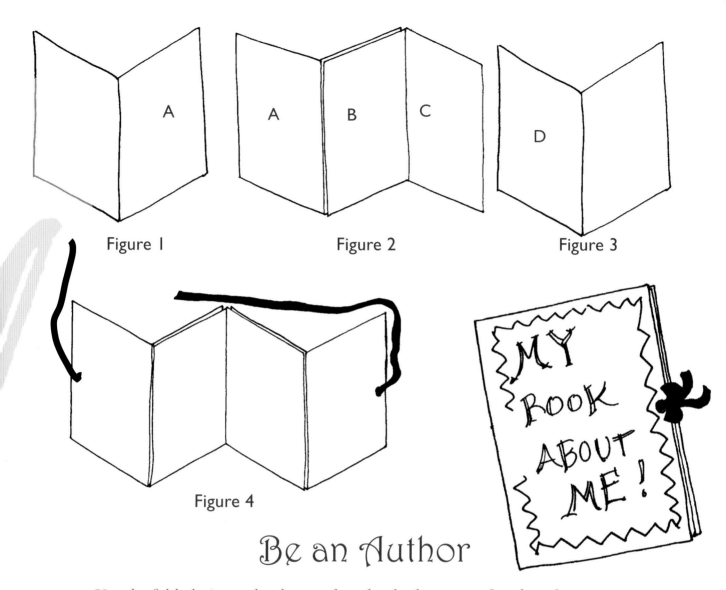

Figure 1

Figure 2

Figure 3

Figure 4

Be an Author

Use the folded picture book to make a book about your family, a favorite trip you took, or an adventure with a pet.

Draw a set of pictures in your book that tell a story about your life since you were a baby. Make it as short or as long as you want. Add photographs or draw pictures to illustrate your story if you like.

Write a story about your family, or a member of your family. Make *Silhouette Portraits (page 133)* of family members for your book.

Little Friendship Book

Make a sweet little gift book from the prettiest scraps of paper you have on hand. Decorate the cover and inside pages with rubber stamps, paint, and markers. Draw special pictures that your friend will enjoy.

MATERIALS NEEDED

Tracing paper

Pencil

Clear tape

Five sheets of 5½-by-8½-inch paper

4-by-4-inch sheet thin cardboard

Scissors

Binder clips

Hole punch

Ribbon or cord, about 12-inches long

1. Assemble all materials on your work surface. Use a pencil to trace or draw the heart shape *(page 63)* on tracing paper and cut out. Tape the pattern to a piece of thin cardboard and outline with a pencil. Use scissors to cut out the heart shape. Set aside.

2. Fold the five sheets of paper in half so the short edges meet. Crease well. Tear or cut paper along the fold. Stack sheets together and clip the sides using binder clips.

3. Tape the cardboard heart on top of stacked paper. Use scissors to cut around the shape. Remove binder clips. You will have ten same-sized paper hearts and one cardboard heart for the top cover.

4. Use binder clips to secure the side edges of the hearts together. Mark symmetrical holes ¼ inch down from the top outer left and right edge. Punch holes through all the layers at the marks. Remove clips.

5. To assemble the book: bring the ribbon end up through one hole and pull through part way. Next, bring the other end up through the other hole. Adjust so the ribbon ends are equal lengths. Tie in a loose bow. (Be sure the bow is loose enough for the pages to be able to open.) Trim ribbon ends if necessary.

5. Decorate the pages and cover of the book with original drawings, rubber stamps, stickers, or watercolor art. Write messages on each page in colored pencil or watercolor paints. Let dry. Wrap in tissue paper and give to a friend.

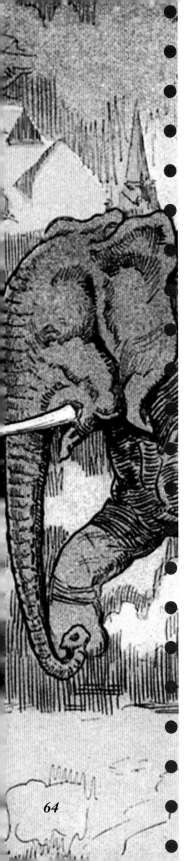

Critter Cutouts

Create a collection of paper animals made out of folded paper.
Color and decorate to use as toys or homemade greeting cards.

MATERIALS NEEDED

8½-by-11-inch sheet of
construction paper for each animal

Pencil

Colored pencils

Scissors

1. Assemble all materials on your work surface. Fold a sheet of 8½-by-11-inch paper in half widthwise so the short edges meet. Press the fold firmly to crease. The paper should measure 5½-by-8½ inches. The folded edge will be along the top.

2. Draw and color a side view outline of the elephant or a favorite animal (Figure 1). Cut out the shape leaving the top fold of the paper uncut (Figure 2). Open and display on table.

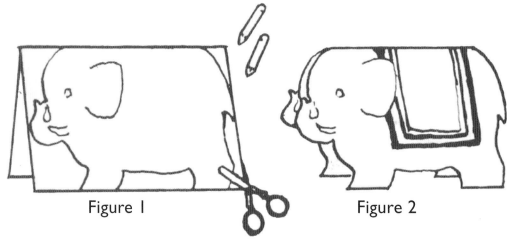

Figure 1   Figure 2

Envelope Animals

If you don't have extra paper to cut, use discarded or leftover stationery envelopes to make a set of circus animal. Try making a circus of animals from various sized envelopes.

MATERIALS NEEDED

One envelope (any size) for each animal

Pencil

Colored pencils

Scissors

1. For each animal use one envelope. If necessary, seal the flap. For a tall animal (like a giraffe) turn the envelope lengthwise, and for a shorter animal (like a cow) turn the envelope widthwise.

2. With your pencil, draw a sideview of your favorite animal on one side the envelope. The top of the figure must touch the fold of the envelope to make the figures two-sided. Color your animals using colored pencils.

3. Use scissors to cut along the outlined shape, leaving the top fold of the envelope uncut. Open and display.

Making Jewelry

Salt Dough Beads

More Play with Salt Dough

Rolled Paper Beads

Button Bracelet

Bottle Cap Pin

Friendship Pin

Reversible Leaf Brooch

Leaf Art Journal

Acorn Jewelry

Owl Badge Pin

Folded Paper Jewelry

Salt Dough Beads

This no-cook salt dough is easy to make and will store well for several days when wrapped and refrigerated. Make different-size beads and pendants to give as gifts.

MATERIALS NEEDED

Large plastic or metal bowl

1 cup flour

1 cup fine salt

½ cup warm water

Poster paint or food coloring

Newspaper, paper bag, or waxed paper

Narrow chopstick or pencil

Paintbrush

Embroidery floss thread or elastic cord

Paperclip or pipe cleaner

1. Assemble all materials on your work surface. In a large bowl, combine the flour and salt and mix well. Add the water and food coloring or paint to the dry ingredients and mix with clean hands until combined.

2. On a clean work surface, knead well until all the flour and salt are combined and the color is even throughout the mixture. The dough should be firm and soft.

3. Roll a small amount of dough in the palm of your hand to form a bead about the size of a small marble. Poke a chopstick or pencil through the center of each bead and twist lightly to form a hole then remove. Set each bead on newspaper and allow to dry overnight.

4. When the beads are dry, paint and decorate as you wish. String beads on embroidery floss or elastic cord to make a necklace or bracelet.

5. To make a pendant from a freshly rolled dough bead, bend a paper clip or a piece of pipe cleaner into a "U" shape. Insert the bottom of the "U" into the dough bead and push both prongs into the dough to make a small loop. Let dry.

6. Thread floss or cord through the loop and tie the ends of the cord in a bow or a knot.

TIP *Make different shaped beads such as ovals, squares, and rectangles.*

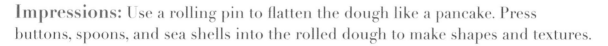

More Play With Salt Dough

*Experiment with different shapes and textures
using natural and household materials.*

Impressions: Use a rolling pin to flatten the dough like a pancake. Press buttons, spoons, and sea shells into the rolled dough to make shapes and textures.

Patterns: Make patterns by pressing objects such as acorns, plastic straws, combs, and craftsticks gently into the surface of the dough. Draw pictures with toothpicks and small twigs. Roll dough onto newspaper then peel off to transfer pictures and letters.

Coils: Roll out the dough into long ropes. Wrap the rope in a spiral around itself (like a snake) to make small plates and bowls.

Shapes: Roll out the dough and cut shapes with cookie cutters or a blunt knife.

Snipping: Use blunt scissors to cut out shapes of trees, fruits, stars and circles.

Rolled Paper Beads

Make rolled paper beads using recycled magazines or decorative paper.
Use your beads to make unique necklaces and bracelets or pins.

MATERIALS NEEDED

Newspaper

Magazine pages or decorative paper

Ruler

Pencil

Scissors

White glue or glue stick

Ribbon or cord

1. Set out the newspaper on your work surface. For each bead, you will need one 1½-by-12 inch strip of magazine or decorative paper. To make one necklace use at least five beads.

2. Using your ruler, draw a diagonal line on each paper strip from the upper left edge to the lower right edge (Figure 1). Use scissors to cut along the dotted line (Figure 2).

3. To roll a bead: Take a pencil and wrap the wide edge of the paper strip around it once. Apply glue along the inside top edge of the paper strip and roll the glued edge into the paper. Continue rolling towards the end of the strip, keeping the paper tight around the pencil as you roll (Figure 3).

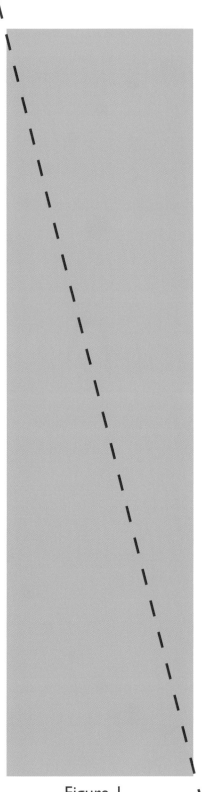

Figure 1

4. When you reach the end of the strip, add a dab of glue to the narrow end of paper. Press the edge firmly to the bead. Slip the bead off the pencil and allow to dry. Repeat as above until you have enough beads to make a necklace or bracelet. String the beads on a ribbon or cord and tie the ends in a bow.

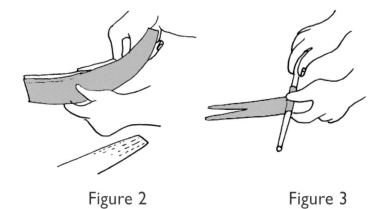

Figure 2

Figure 3

TIP *Try these other paper cuts for a variety of paper bead shapes.*

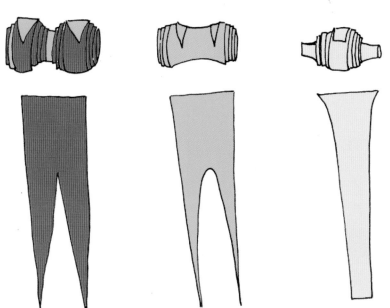

71

Button Bracelet

Make a pretty bracelet from two-hole buttons. Be sure to store your button collection in a recycled box or jar (see page 11).

MATERIALS NEEDED

Two-hole buttons, variety of shapes and colors

Beads

Tray

Needle

Hemp string

1. Assemble all materials on your work surface. Spread your button collection on a tray and choose a handful of your favorite shapes and colors. Choose buttons with holes large enough to fit the thickness of your string. Arrange the selected buttons in a pattern that you like before you begin to sew.

2. Measure and cut a length of hemp string by wrapping it around your wrist. Add 6 inches to this length to making a closing.

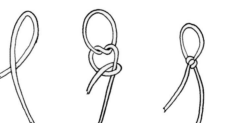

Figure 1

3. To make a closing: First select a small button (or bead) to use as your end button. The size of the button will determine the size of your loop. Next, fold one end of the string over to form a small loop. Tie the bottom of the folded loop in a knot (Figure 1). Adjust your loop to fit your button if necessary.

4. Thread the other end of string through the needle. Pull the needle up through the first button hole then weave the end back down through the second hole. Pull the thread through gently and slide the button along the string until you reach the end knot. Continue sewing on the rest of the buttons as below (Figure 2).

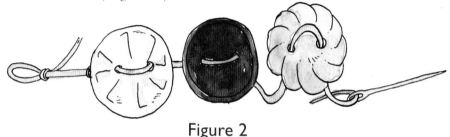

Figure 2

5. Adjust each button to lay flat and even with the previous button. (It's ok if the buttons overlap a bit.) Continue to thread each button until you are ready to add the small end button. When you have threaded the last button, tie the end of the string in a knot, close to the back of the button (Figure 3). Trim thread and try on your bracelet by slipping end button through the loop at the other end. Adjust size if necessary by retying the loop.

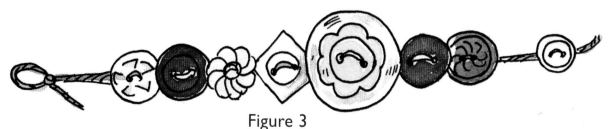

Figure 3

Bottle Cap Pin

Use metal bottle caps to make custom art pins using favorite pictures and homemade art. Collect and trade bottle cap pins with friends.

MATERIALS NEEDED

Metal soda bottle cap, one for each pin

Magazine or decorative paper

Scissors

White glue

Pinback (found in most craft stores)

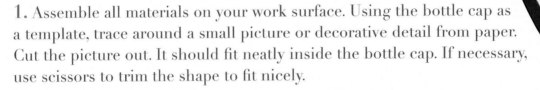

1. Assemble all materials on your work surface. Using the bottle cap as a template, trace around a small picture or decorative detail from paper. Cut the picture out. It should fit neatly inside the bottle cap. If necessary, use scissors to trim the shape to fit nicely.

2. Apply glue to the backside of the picture and place it, glued side down, inside the bottle cap. Press well to smooth out the picture. If it doesn't stick, let it sit a few more minutes. Be careful not to over glue! Dab glue along the inside edges of the cap and add small beads and glitter as decoration. Glue the pin back to the back of the bottle cap. Let it dry overnight before wearing.

Friendship Pin

This is a perfect rainy day project. These simple pins make wonderful gifts for special friends. Use your imagination to create many different designs.

MATERIALS NEEDED

Safety pins, assorted-sizes

Rolled Paper Beads (page 70)

Small containers or bowls

Assorted colorful beads

Tray

1. Assemble all materials on your work surface. Set out *Rolled Paper Beads* (*page 70*) and a small bowl of beads on a tray.

2. For each pin, take a safety pin and carefully open the clasp. Slip on several small beads, one large paper bead, and then several more small beads. That's it! Pin on shirt or close clasp to store.

 You can also try sliding on buttons as well as beads to make a colorful pin.

Reversible Leaf Brooch

Make a two-sided leaf brooch to wear for different occasions. Draw the stem and structure of the leaf on felt and use the Stem Stitch (page 25) to outline the detail. Collect leaves (see Leaf Art Journal, page 77), and design a variety of leaf pins.

MATERIALS NEEDED

Pencil

Tracing paper

Straight pins

One piece of green felt

One piece of yellow felt

Scissors

Needle

Embroidery floss
(yellow, red, or orange)

Safety pin (medium size)

OAK

1. Assemble all materials on your work surface. Using a pencil, trace the outline of a leaf onto tracing paper and cut out. You can use the pattern on this page, or a fresh leaf.

2. Stack the green felt on top of the yellow felt. Pin the leaf pattern to the felt. Using scissors, cut around the edge of the leaf pattern. Remove the pattern and repin the fabric together.

3. Thread your needle and tie a knot in the end. Using the *Up-and-Down Stitch (page 23)*, or the *Blanket Stitch (page 27)*, sew the edges together in small, even stitches. When finished, remove pins and attach a safety pin on either side. Attach to shirt. To reverse, remove the safety pin and repin to the other side.

Leaf Art Journal

Make a journal in which you can draw and record your collections and notes about the plants and leaves in your area. Use the leaf designs for other projects such as the Embroidered Pillowcase (page 37), or Reversible Leaf Brooch (page 76).

MATERIALS NEEDED

Blank notebook (pocket-size)

Colored pencils

Drawing pencil

Tree identification guide

Clear tape

1. To get started, you will need a blank notebook, colored pencils, and a good drawing pencil. Ask a librarian to help you find a tree identification book.

2. Learn to identify leaves in your area by collecting specimens throughout the year. Press leaves between clean pages in the journal. Tape the leaf stem onto the page to help keep it in place.

3. Next to the leaf, write a brief description about it. Notice what characterizes the leaf; the edges, the stems, the shape, or the size. Will these details help you recognize the leaf on a walk? Draw a picture of the leaf structure. Use colored pencils to add color and detail to your drawing.

Acorn Jewelry

*Make decorative necklaces and bracelets using
fresh acorns. The best time to collect acorns, either from the tree or
on the ground, is when they begin falling, usually in late August.*

MATERIALS NEEDED

Small bag or Placemat Roll-Up Pouch (page 38)

Old bread board (for pounding)

Acorns

Small hammer

Small nail with head

Large-eye needle

Heavy string, about 18 inches long

Colored beads

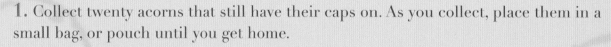

1. Collect twenty acorns that still have their caps on. As you collect, place them in a small bag, or pouch until you get home.

2. Assemble all materials on your work surface. Working on the surface of the bread board, gently pound the nail through the side of the acorn, just beneath the cap to make a hole. Be careful not to crack the acorn as you pound. Make holes in as many acorns as you need.

3. Thread your needle with 14 inches of string, leaving a 2-inch tail on both sides for tying. Tie a knot in one end. Push the needle and thread through a hole in one acorn, pushing it back to the end knot. Next, add three colored beads. Continue stringing, alternating acorns with the beads until you reach the end. Tie the two ends in a bow and try on your necklace.

Owl Badge

Felt badges are a great craft project for groups. Create a sewing club and ask friends to join.

MATERIALS NEEDED

Pencil

Tracing paper

Scissors

Pins

Felt (two pieces)

Large-eye needle

Embroidery floss

Safety pin (medium size)

CUT ONE

1. Assemble all materials on your work surface. Use a pencil to outline the circle on tracing paper. Cut out the circle. Next, trace or draw a picture of an owl (above left) on tracing paper, making sure it fits inside the circle. Cut out the owl and set aside.

2. Pin the circle pattern onto a piece of felt and cut out. With a pencil, draw a simple circle on the inside edge of the felt. Sew along the outline using the *Up-and-Down Stitch (page 23)* and embroidery floss.

3. Next, pin the owl pattern onto a different color of felt and cut out. Remove the pattern and position the owl in the center of the felt circle. Pin in place. Sew onto the felt circle using the *Chain Stitch (page 29)* and embroidery floss. When done, secure a safety pin to the back and pin onto your shirt or favorite bag.

TIP   *Before sewing the owl onto the circle, use the French Knot (page 30) to make eyes and the Stem Stitch (page 25) to outline the feet. Add other details as you wish.*

Folded Paper Jewelry

You don't need glue or tape to make fanciful folded paper shapes used for these necklaces and bracelets. Vary the size of the loops by cutting the arch shorter, or by using a larger piece of folded paper.

MATERIALS NEEDED

Recycled magazine pages, maps, decorative paper

1. To begin, cut six 3-by-6-inch strips out of the recycled paper.

2. For each loop, fold one strip of paper in half so the short edges meet. Press to crease. Next, fold the lower edge up to the meet the top. Press the fold firmly to crease. (You should now have folds on the left and bottom of the folded paper (Figure 1).

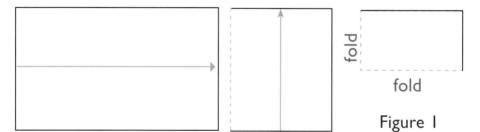

fold

fold

Figure 1

3. Draw or cut an arch shape (Figure 2). Each end of the arch must fall on the fold for the link to work properly. Hold paper firmly and cut out along the lines. Do not cut through the folded edges. Unfold the loop to view. (Figure 3).

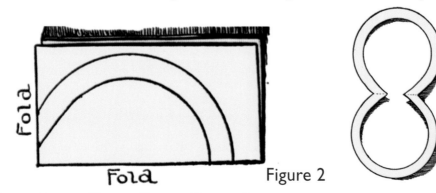

Fold

Fold

Figure 2

Figure 3

4. To make a necklace or bracelet: Start with the open link and slide a folded link over one end to look like Figure 4. Next, slide another folded link over the other end of the open link to look like Figure 5. Continue adding links evenly to each end until you have the desired length.

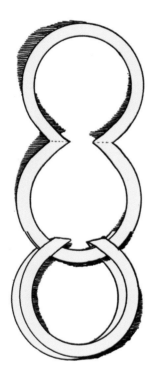

Figure 4

Figure 5

5. To fasten the chain together, cut a paper tab in the shape of Figure 6. Make the slit large enough for the pointed tip to slide through. Fasten to the end loops and close (Figure 7).

Figure 6

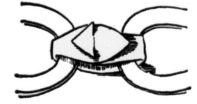

Figure 7

Baking

Baking Basics
Irish Soda Bread
Popovers
Busy Morning Biscuits
Cheese Pizza
Baked Pretzels
Olive Oil Bread
Double-Crust Pie Dough
Decorative Edging
Peach Pie
Pinwheels
Little Blueberry Tarts
Sunshine Cake
Mix-and-Match Frosting
Simple Decorations
Fancy Cupcakes
Sugar Cookie Cut-Outs
Colored Sugar
Cookie Icing Paint

Baking Basics

Read the recipe carefully from start to finish before you begin. Check to be sure that you have all ingredients on hand.

Be sure you have enough time to finish the recipe. Making bread, for example, takes a few hours.

Wash your hands with warm soap and water before handling ingredients. Have all of your ingredients out on your workspace, measured, and prepared before you begin to bake.

Only bake or cook with an adult in the house. Never leave the kitchen when using the stove or oven.

Use dry potholders or oven mitts when setting baking sheets into the oven and when removing them.

Preheat oven for at least 15 minutes before baking.

Do not put a pan in an oven that is not fully preheated or you risk having a crust form on the top of the baked item too quickly.

Always set the baking rack in the middle of the oven for the baking projects in this book.

Try to avoid opening the oven door while baking. When you open the door, it allows the heat to escape. The rapid rise and fall of heat in the oven may cause your item to cook unevenly.

For baked goods, use glass pans or heavy metal pans.

Baking Equipment

Apron or smock

Baking pans
  baking pan (8- and 9-inch square)
  baking sheet
  cake pan (8-inch round)
  bread loaf pan
  muffin pan
  pie pan
  popover pan

Bowls, metal and plastic

Colander

Cutting board

Electric mixer

Kitchen timer

Knives (for making pie dough)

Paring knife

Measuring cups (glass for liquid, and plastic or metal for dry ingredients)

Measuring spoons

Metal cooling rack

Mixing spoons

Oven mitts or potholders

Pastry brush

Pastry cloth or waxed paper (for rolling dough)

Rubber spatula

Pancake spatula

Vegetable peeler

Wire whisk

Rolling pin

Basic Baking Ingredients

Brown sugar

Granulated sugar

Confectioners' sugar (powdered sugar)

Honey

Unsalted butter (organic if possible)

Oil (vegetable oil or olive oil)

Eggs (free roaming or organic)

Milk (2% unless otherwise indicated)

All-purpose flour

Whole-wheat flour

Active dry yeast

Salt

Baking powder

Baking soda

Vanilla extract

Baking Extras

Aluminum foil

Paper muffin cup liners

Parchment paper

Waxed paper

Wooden toothpicks

Baking Terms

Bake To cook food in a hot oven

Batter A measure of liquid, flour, and other possible ingredients that are thin enough to pour

Beat To stir quickly and repeatedly until a mixture of flour and liquid is combined

Blend To mix foods together thoroughly with a wooden spoon, electric mixer or wire whisk

Chill To cool an ingredient in the refrigerator until it is cold

Chop To cut food into smaller pieces with a sharp knife

Coat To cover an ingredient with a thin outer layer, such as flour, sugar, or spices

Combine To stir two or more ingredients together until they are mixed well and do not separate

Cool To let food stand at room temperature until no longer hot

Cream To mix one or more foods (usually butter and sugar) with a spoon or an electric mixer until soft and creamy

Fold To gently cut down through batter with a spatula or spoon to mix in a light ingredient such as egg whites or butter.

Frost To cover or decorate a cake or cookie with frosting or icing

Grease To rub the surface of a pan or dish with butter or oil to prevent food from sticking.

Icing A sugary mixture used to cover cakes (see **Frost**)

Knead To push and fold dough until smooth, and elastic

Level To make even and flat, such as a level cup of flour

Lukewarm A temperature (normally referring to a liquid) that is neither cold nor hot

Mix To combine two or more ingredients by stirring with a spoon or using an electric mixer

Peel To strip off the outer covering or skin of fruit such as apples or peaches

Preheat To heat an oven to a desired temperature before placing dish in the oven to cook

Proof To dissolve yeast in a warm liquid until it becomes bubbly and starts to expand

Punch Down To press down the bread dough after it rises.

Rise When yeast and flour expand together to form dough

Stir To mix with a spoon in a circular or rotating motion

Whisk To quickly beat ingredients with a fork, wire whisk, or mixer until they are light and fluffy

How to Measure Ingredients

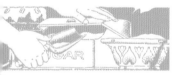

To Measure Dry Ingredients:
Use graduated measuring cups (¼ cup, ½ cup and 1 cup) or graduated measuring spoons (¼ teaspoon, ½ teaspoon, 1 teaspoon, 1 tablespoon) to measure dry ingredients such as flour, sugar, cocoa powder, baking soda, and salt as well as liquid ingredients such as oil and butter.

Measure baking powder and baking soda exactly. Fill a measuring spoon heaping full and use the straight edge of a butter knife to level off.

To measure flour or granulated sugar, lightly spoon the flour into the graduated measuring cup. Use the straight edge of a butter knife to level off even with the top.

To measure melted butter, first melt the butter, then measure by level tablespoons.

To measure liquids such as milk, water, juice, and oil use liquid measuring cups. These come with 1 cup, 2 cup, 4 cup, and 8 cup measurements.

To measure a baking sheet or baking pan use a ruler to measure the top from the inside for length, and width. To measure the depth, place the ruler on the inside base and measure the side from the bottom to the top.

Irish Soda Bread

Breakfast on the weekend never has to be dull with this quick batter bread.
Serve with honey or jam and a big pot of peppermint tea.

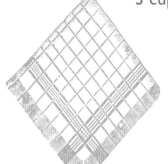

3 cups all-purpose flour, plus more for kneading

¾ cup whole-wheat flour

1 teaspoon baking soda

1 teaspoon salt

1¾ cups buttermilk (more if needed)

1. Set the rack in the middle of the oven. Preheat oven to 425 degrees. Lightly grease a baking sheet. Set aside.

2. In a large bowl, combine the all-purpose and whole-wheat flour, baking soda, and salt. Stir to mix well. Pour in buttermilk and stir with a wooden spoon until the batter is moistened. (Add a small handful of all-purpose flour if your dough is too sticky.)

3. Place batter on a floured surface and knead lightly to form a smooth dough-ball. Pat the dough into a round shape and place it on the baking sheet. Using a sharp knife, cut a cross shape into the batter about 1-inch deep. Bake for 45 minutes.

4. Using oven mitts, remove the pan from the oven and place on a wire rack to cool. To test that the bread is fully baked, turn the bread round on its side and tap the bottom. It will sound hollow when done. Serve warm with fresh jam or honey.

Makes one round of bread

TIP *To store, cover the bread in a tea towel and lightly sprinkle a few drops of water on top of the cloth to keep the bread moist.*

Popovers

*It's always a thrill to see popovers bake high in their little cups.
These are perfect anytime you want a freshly baked treat.*

3 eggs

1 cup milk

1 cup all-purpose flour

½ teaspoon salt

1. Set the rack in the middle of the oven. Preheat oven to 400 degrees. Generously grease popover pan or oven-proof glass baking cups. (If you are using glass baking cups, set them on a baking sheet, evenly spaced and not touching.) Set aside.

2. In a medium bowl, whisk the eggs until frothy. Add milk and stir until combined.

3. Using a fork, slowly add the flour and salt, mixing just until the batter is smooth and well blended. (Be careful not to over mix.)

4. Use a small measuring cup, pour the batter into the popover cups, filling halfway. Set the popover pan in the oven and bake for 30 minutes or until golden brown and very puffy. Using oven mitts, remove the pan from the oven and place on a wire rack to cool. Remove popovers from the pan and serve warm with your favorite jam.

Makes six popovers

Busy Morning Biscuits

Learning to roll dough is a rite of passage for new bakers. These biscuits are a good afterschool project, but can be enjoyed any time of day.

4 cups all-purpose flour, plus more for kneading

3½ teaspoons baking powder

½ teaspoon salt

1¾ cup buttermilk

¼ cup (4 tablespoons) melted butter or vegetable oil

1. Set the rack in the middle of the oven. Preheat oven to 450 degrees. Lightly grease a 8-inch square baking pan. Set aside.

2. In a large bowl, combine flour, baking powder, and salt.

3. Use your hands to form a well in the center of the flour and pour in the buttermilk and melted butter or oil. Mix until well combined and soft. Gently mold dough into a ball.

4. Sprinkle flour on a large cutting board or clean counter and spread the dough out with your hands. Press down on the dough ball with the palms of your hands to flatten. Lightly press the dough away from you. Next, fold the dough back towards you and give it a one-quarter turn clockwise (right to left). Knead lightly, about ten times, until the dough holds together. (Add a small handful of flour if your dough is too sticky.)

5. Using a rolling pin, lightly roll the dough out to a ½-inch thickness. Place a glass or 2-inch round cookie cutter onto the dough and press firmly to make a cut circle. Set the cut circles close together in the baking pan, about 1 inch apart.

6. Bake for 12 minutes or until golden brown. Using oven mitts, remove the pan from the oven and place on a wire rack to cool. Serve warm.

Make 12 to 14 biscuits

Cheese Pizza

Declare every Friday night homemade pizza night! The smell of my mom's pizza drifting through the house will make any kitchen the happiest place on earth.

1 package active dry yeast

5 tablespoon warm water

¼ teaspoon honey

1 cup milk or water

3 tablespoons olive oil, plus 1 teaspoon for greasing

1 teaspoon salt

3 cups all-purpose flour, plus more for kneading

Topping:

1 cup tomato sauce (store bought or homemade)

2 tablespoons olive oil

2 cups of mozzarella, grated

Fresh basil leaves, torn into small pieces

1. Set the rack in the middle of the oven. Preheat oven to 450 degrees. Lightly grease two pizza pans or baking sheets. Set aside.

2. In a large bowl, stir together yeast, warm water, and honey. Whisk to combine. Let the yeast bubble for up to five minutes. Using a wooden spoon, stir milk or water, olive oil and salt into the yeast mixture. Gradually stir in flour until combined.

3. Sprinkle flour on a large cutting board or clean counter and spread the dough out with your hands. Press down on the dough ball with the palms of your hands. Lightly press the dough away from you. Next, fold the dough back towards you and give it a one-quarter turn clockwise. Knead lightly, about ten times, until the dough holds together. (Add a small handful of flour if your dough is too sticky.)

4. Set the dough in a lightly oiled bowl. Gently turn the dough in the bowl to coat it with a thin layer of olive oil. Cover with clean dish towel or plate and set in a warm area to rise until doubled in size, about 45 minutes.

5. When the dough is ready, punch down gently to flatten. Pressing with your fingers, shape it into a 12-inch circle. Transfer onto a pizza pan or baking sheet.

6. Drizzle the olive oil onto the dough. Spoon the tomato sauce in an even layer across the dough. Distribute cheese evenly on the surface. Sprinkle the top with salt, pepper, and bits of basil leaves.

7. Bake for twenty minutes, or until the cheese is bubbling and the crust is crisp and golden. Using oven mitts, remove the pan from the oven and place on a wire rack to cool for five minutes. Cut the pizza into wedges and serve right away.

Makes two twelve-inch pizzas

Baked Pretzels

The pretzel shape is considered a symbol of good luck and prosperity.
These easy baked pretzels are a perfect rainy day project.

1 package active dry yeast

1 cup warm water

1 tablespoon honey

2 tablespoons light olive oil

½ teaspoon salt

2¼ cups all-purpose flour, plus
more for kneading

½ cup whole-wheat flour

1 egg

1 tablespoon water

Salt for sprinkling

1. Set the rack in the middle of the oven. Preheat oven to 375 degrees. Lightly grease two baking sheets. Set aside.

2. In a large bowl, stir together warm water, yeast, and honey. Whisk to combine. Let the yeast bubble for up to five minutes. Using a wooden spoon, stir olive oil and salt into the yeast mixture. Gradually stir in the all-purpose and whole-wheat flour until combined.

3. Sprinkle all-purpose flour on a large cutting board or clean counter and spread the dough out with your hands. Press down on the dough ball with the palms of your hands. Lightly press the dough away from you. Next, fold the

dough back towards you and give it a one-quarter turn clockwise. Knead lightly, about ten times, until the dough holds together. (Add a small handful of flour if your dough is too sticky.)

4. Set the dough in a lightly oiled bowl. Gently turn the dough in the bowl to coat it with a thin layer of olive oil. Cover with clean dish towel or plate and set in a warm area to rise until doubled in size, about 45 minutes.

5. When the dough is ready, punch down gently to flatten. Divide the dough into sixteen equal pieces. Roll each piece with your palm to make a stick about 18-inches long and the diameter of a pencil. Shape the dough in an arch and bring the ends up to cross one end over the other. Press down the ends so the dough sticks together.

6. In a small bowl, combine the egg and water. Whisk well. Using a pastry brush, coat each pretzel with the egg mixture, and sprinkle lightly with salt. Place on baking sheet and bake for 20 minutes or until golden brown. Using oven mitts, remove the pan from the oven. Use a spatula to transfer warm pretzels to the rack and let them cool completely.

Makes 16 pretzels

Olive Oil Bread

This is a kid-friendly bread recipe and perfect for beginner bakers. It requires minimal kneading. You can start it after school and it will be ready at dinner time.

I package active dry yeast

I cup warm water

4 tablespoons olive oil

I teaspoon salt

I tablespoon of finely chopped fresh rosemary, (optional)

2 cups all-purpose flour, plus more for kneading

I cup whole-wheat flour

1. Set the rack in the middle of the oven. Preheat oven to 425 degrees. Lightly grease a baking sheet. Set aside. In a large bowl, stir together yeast, warm water, olive oil, salt, and rosemary. Whisk to combine. Let the yeast bubble for up to five minutes. Use a wooden spoon to stir in flour gradually and mix until combined.

2. Sprinkle flour on a large cutting board or clean counter and spread the dough out with your hands. Press down on the dough ball with the palms of your hands. Lightly press the dough away from you. Next, fold the dough back towards you and give it a one-quarter turn clockwise. Knead lightly, about ten times, until the dough holds together. (Add a small handful of flour if your dough is too sticky.)

3. Set the dough in a lightly oiled bowl. Gently turn the dough in the bowl to coat it with a thin layer of olive oil. Cover with clean dish towel or plate and set in a warm area to rise until doubled in size, about 45 minutes.

4. When the dough is ready, punch it down and roll into an oval or a round loaf. Place on baking sheet. Let the dough rest for about 20 minutes and then bake for 25 minutes or until golden brown. Using oven mitts, remove the pan from the oven and place on a wire rack to cool. Enjoy!

Makes one oval or round loaf

Double-crust Pie Dough

*Once you make a double-crust homemade pie, you may just want to
make a variety of fruit pies throughout the year!*

3 cups all-purpose flour

I teaspoon salt

I cup (two sticks) cold, unsalted butter

½ cup ice-cold water

1. Set out a 9-inch pie pan. Combine flour and salt in mixing bowl. Cut in butter with two knives until the mixture is the consistency of coarse cornmeal.

2. Sprinkle the cold water, one tablespoon at a time, into the flour mixture. Toss the mixture lightly and stir with a fork. Add water to the driest part and continue to mix until the dough is moist enough to hold together when pressed gently with a fork.

3. Shape the dough into two equal-sized balls. Set one dough ball on a floured work surface and press into a flat circle with your hands.

4. To make a bottom crust: Using your rolling pin, roll the dough in light short strokes from the center in all directions to an ¼-inch thickness (or slightly less), making an 11-inch circle. Fold the rolled dough in half over the rolling pin. Ease it loosely into the pie pan with the fold in the center.

5. Unfold the dough and fit it into the pan. (Be careful not to stretch the dough.) Gently press out air pockets and pinch together broken edges with your fingertips. Using a butter knife, trim off the extra dough so it is even with the top edge of the pie pan. Lightly prick the inside bottom of the crust with a fork.

6. To make a top crust: Roll out the second ball of dough just as you did for the bottom crust.

7. Place the filling *(page 97)* in the center of the lined pie pan and spread evenly with a fork. Fold top crust in half over the rolling pin and place it on top of the pie with fold in center. Gently unfold the dough over the top of pie.

8. Using a butter knife, trim off the extra dough leaving ½ inch over the edge of the pie pan. Fold the edges under the bottom crust and pinch gently with fingers to seal. (The pinching will help to make an upright crust edge.)

9. Using a fork or a butter knife, gently prick a pattern or a shape on the top to allow the steam to escape.

Decorative Edging

You can make a variety of decorative pie edges once you have pinched the top and bottom crusts together. Try one of the following ideas:

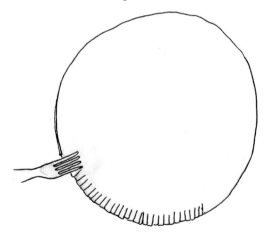

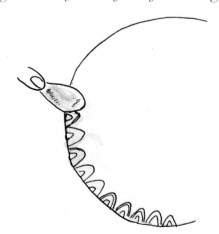

1. Press the tip of a fork to make evenly spaced imprints around the edge of the pie crust.

2. Press the tip of a spoon to make evenly spaced scalloped imprints around the edge of the pie crust.

Peach Pie

Peach pie is best when made with freshly picked ripe peaches.
Top with vanilla ice cream for a special treat.

Double-crust Pie Dough (page 95)

5 cups fresh, sliced peaches

¾ cup granulated sugar

3 tablespoons all-purpose flour

½ teaspoon cinnamon

2 tablespoon unsalted cold butter

1. Set the rack in the middle of the oven. Preheat oven to 425 degrees.

2. Roll out one disk of pie dough (page 95). Fold the rolled dough in half over the rolling pin. Ease it loosely into the 9-inch pie pan with the fold in the center. Trim any excess dough along the edges with a blunt knife or pinch into small scallops. Chill in freezer for about ten minutes while you make the filling.

3. Cut peaches in half. Use a paring knife to take off the skin and remove the pit. Cut halves into quarters, and then cut each quarter into 3 even slices.

4. In a medium bowl, combine sugar, flour, and cinnamon. Add peaches and stir gently with a fork to evenly coat the peaches with the mixture. Fill the pie pan with peach mixture and dot with butter pieces.

5. Cover with a top crust *(page 96)* and lightly prick the crust with a fork. Set in oven and bake for 10 minutes, then *reduce heat* to 350 degrees and bake for 35 minutes or until the crust is golden brown. Using oven mitts, remove the pie from the oven and place on a wire rack to cool. Serve warm.

Makes one 9-inch pie

Pinwheels

Make tasty pinwheels using pie dough. Fill with jam or sprinkle generously with cinnamon and sugar (see recipe below in TIP). These are perfect for tea parties!

| Figure 1 | Figure 2 | Figure 3 |

1. Set out a baking sheet. Roll out one disc of pie dough *(page 95)* ¼-inch thick (or slightly less). Use a blunt knife to cut 4-inch squares from the dough. Next, cut a line from each corner almost to the center of the square. Fill the center with a teaspoon of jam or a generous sprinkling of cinnamon and sugar (Figure 1).

2. Working clockwise (right to left), fold the top right corner into the center of the dough and press lightly (Figure 2). Continue to overlap each corner in the center and press well (Figure 3).

3. Place each pinwheel on the cookie sheet. Set in oven and bake for 10 minutes or until the crust is golden brown. Using oven mitts, remove the pie from the oven and place on a wire rack to cool. Serve warm.

TIP *Making a batch of cinnamon and sugar is easy. Just mix 4 teaspoons of sugar and ¼ teaspoon of ground cinnamon in a small bowl. Stir to combine and sprinkle onto dough before folding corners. Store extra mixture in a small lidded jar.*

Little Blueberry Tarts

Make little tarts using a muffin tin instead of a pie pan.
Pick a favorite fruit filling and serve as an everyday treat.

Pie dough (page 95)

Butter for greasing

2½ cups fresh blueberries

¼ cup granulated sugar

½ teaspoon lemon juice

1½ tablespoons all-purpose flour

1. Set the rack in the middle of the oven. Preheat oven to 350 degrees. Set out a 12 cup muffin pan and set aside. Lightly grease the cups with butter.

2. Roll out one disk of pie dough and use a drinking glass or cookie cutter to cut circles in the dough. Set the cut dough into muffin cups. Gently press dough into the sides to smooth out air bubbles. Trim any excess dough along the edges with a blunt knife or pinch into small scallops. Chill in freezer for ten minutes while you make the filling.

3. **To make the filling:** In a large bowl, combine blueberries, sugar, lemon juice, and flour. Stir gently to coat the berries evenly. Set aside.

4. Take the muffins pan from the freezer and fill each tart with a heaping spoonful of berry mixture. Bake for 15 minutes, or until the crust is golden brown and the juices are bubbling. Using oven mitts, remove the pan from the oven and place on a wire rack to cool. To loosen the tarts from the muffin pan, run a butter knife along the inside edges of the cups. Serve warm.

Makes 12 tarts.

Sunshine Cake

It's always good to have a cake recipe that can be turned into cupcakes for a children's party or a rainy weekend activity. Use this recipe to make a birthday cake or cupcakes for the special day!

½ cup (one stick) butter, softened

1 cup granulated sugar

3 eggs

1 teaspoon vanilla extract

2 cups all-purpose flour

2 teaspoons baking powder

¼ teaspoon salt

¾ cup milk

2 tablespoons rainbow sprinkles
(optional)

1. Set the rack in the middle of the oven. Preheat oven to 375 degrees. Line 24 muffins cups with paper liners or grease well an 8-inch round cake pan.

2. In a large bowl, using a wooden spoon or an electric mixer, beat the butter and sugar until light and fluffy. Add the eggs and vanilla then beat until smooth. In a small bowl, whisk together flour, baking powder, and salt.

3. Add half the flour mixture to butter mixture and beat until combined. Pour in milk slowly until mixed. Beat in the remaining flour mixture until the batter is smooth. (Fold in rainbow sprinkles at this time, if you wish.)

4. Pour batter into a cake pan or use a small measuring cup to fill each muffin cup half full. Bake for 20 minutes, or until a toothpick inserted in the center comes out clean. Using oven mitts, remove the pan from the oven and place on a wire rack to cool completely. Remove the cake or cupcakes from the pan and frost with *Mix-and-Match Frosting (page 102)*.

Makes one 8-inch round cake or 24 cupcakes

Mix-and-Match Frosting

This basic buttercream frosting is easy to make and delicious on cakes!
Use the color chart below as a guide for mixing and matching colors.

4 cups confectioners' sugar

½ cup (one stick) butter, softened

2 or 3 tablespoons milk

1 teaspoon vanilla extract

Food color (natural food colors can be
found at specialty stores)

1. In a large bowl, using a wooden spoon or an electric mixer, beat together confectioners' sugar, and butter until creamy.

2. Add milk and vanilla and mix until smooth and fluffy. Add a drop or two of food coloring and mix until combined. Spread over cooled cake or cupcakes with a butter knife or rubber spatula.

TIP *To make several bowls of colored frosting divide mixture into small bowls and mix-and-match food coloring as you wish.*

If your frosting seems too thin, stir in more sugar to thicken, and if too thick, add more milk.

Simple Decorations

You don't have to use a store-bought pastry bag to decorate your cake and cupcakes. Make a homemade pastry bag from an envelope or parchment paper.

Letter-size envelope (unused) or parchment paper

Scissors

Mix-and-Match Frosting (page 102)

1. To make an envelope pastry bag: Use scissors to snip off part of the lower left corner of a clean envelope.

2. To make a pastry bag from parchment paper: Cut an 8½-by-11-inch sheet of parchment paper in half diagonally. Roll it into the shape of a cone and use scissors to snip off the bottom point.

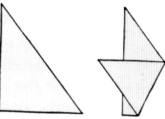

3. To decorate with frosting: Fill the envelope or cone with frosting and press lightly near the bottom until frosting comes out of the tip. Make decorative shapes and letters onto your cupcakes or cake. Try making some of the decorations below or invent your own designs.

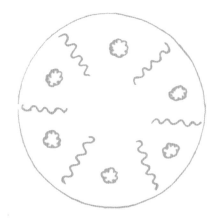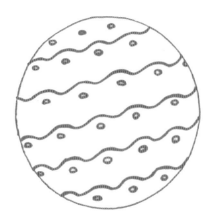

You're Sweet!

You're my favorite cupcake!

I love you!

Fancy Cupcakes

Decorating cupcakes at home doesn't have to be just for birthdays. Invite some friends over to bake and decorate during the weekend or a holiday.

Make assorted bowls of colored frosting from the *Mix-and-Match Frosting* recipe *(page 102)*. Frost each cupcake using a different color.

Create shapes and faces using candies such as jellybeans, gumdrops, sprinkles, licorice sticks, tiny marshmallows or small hard candies.

Make patterns and borders using fruit fresh such as strawberries, blueberries, raspberries.

Use a vegetable peeler to make thin shavings from a solid chocolate bar.

Use an envelope or homemade pastry bag *(page 103)* to make flowers, letters, and simple borders.

Dip animal crackers in melted sweet chocolate and press into the frosting.

Tie a fancy ribbon around the paper cup.

Tape or poke a small piece of paper through a toothpick to make a flag.

Use watercolor to paint a paper doily. Let dry. Set a cupcake on the doily before serving.

Sugar Cookie Cut-Outs

Sugar cookies are not just for a holidays! These delicious treats can be decorated for any occasion. Wrap and give as gifts or enjoy as a homemade treat.
Use store bought cookie cutters or a clean drinking glass to make pleasing shapes.

½ cup (one stick) butter, softened

¾ cup granulated sugar

2 eggs

1 teaspoon vanilla extract

2 cups all-purpose flour

1 ½ teaspoons baking powder

½ teaspoon salt

1. Set the rack in the middle of the oven. Preheat oven to 375 degrees. Lightly grease two baking sheets and set aside.

2. In a large bowl, using a wooden spoon or electric mixer, beat butter and sugar until creamy. Add eggs and vanilla and mix until smooth and fluffy.

3. In a separate bowl, add the flour, baking powder, and salt. Whisk to mix well. Gradually stir flour mixture into the butter mixture until thoroughly combined. Cover the bowl with a clean dish towel or plate and chill in refrigerator for 15 minutes or until firm.

4. Remove the chilled dough and let it soften for 5 to 10 minutes. With clean hands, shape dough into a ball and set the dough on a lightly floured surface. Use a rolling pin to make light, short strokes in all directions across the dough. Roll until the dough is a ¼-inch thickness.

5. To make shapes, dip a cookie cutter or clean drinking glass lightly in flour, and then press firmly into the dough. Carefully pull the cookie cutter off the dough. With a spatula, transfer cookies onto the prepared baking sheets as you go. Set each cookie about 2 inches apart until the baking sheets are full. Bake for 10 minutes or until golden brown.

6. Using oven mitts, remove the baking sheet from the oven and place on a wire rack to cool for three minutes. Use a spatula to transfer warm cookies to the wire rack and cool completely. Decorate with *Colored Sugar (page 108)* or *Cookie Icing Paint (page 109)* if desired.

Makes about 24 cookies

TIP *If you don't have cookie cutters or want to make your own design, cut a shape from a cereal box. Lay the cardboard template on top of the dough and use a blunt knife to trim around the shape.*

Colored Sugar

For an extra bit of dazzle, decorate your cookies with homemade colored sugar.

3 drops food coloring

3 drops of water

¼ cup granulated sugar

2 tablespoons light corn syrup (for painting)

Small paintbrush

Small plate (for dipping)

1. In a small glass, mix food coloring and water together. Measure ¼ cup of sugar into a separate small bowl.

2. Start by adding one drop of food coloring mixture to the sugar. Press with a fork to combine. Add one or two more drops of mixture until sugar is the desired color. Pour colored sugar into a small plate.

3. Pour corn syrup into another small plate. Dip paintbrush in the corn syrup, and paint decorative patterns along the top edge of the cookie (or across the whole surface).

4. Hold the cookie along the edges. Press the top surface of the cookie upside down into the plate of sugar. (The sugar will stick to the painted pattern.) Shake lightly over the plate and return cookie to the cooling rack or a serving plate.

Cookie Icing Paint

Use icing to "paint" your cookies like a true artist!

I cup sifted confectioners' sugar

¼ teaspoon salt

½ teaspoon vanilla

I tablespoon water

Food coloring

Pastry brush or paintbrush

1. In a small bowl, add confectioners' sugar and salt and mix to combine. Add vanilla and water then stir until the cookie paint mixture is easy to spread.

2. Set out a small bowl or plate—one for each color. Add two or three tablespoons of cookie paint mixture and a few drops of food coloring to each bowl or plate. Stir until the color is evenly distributed. Add more water if it is too thick and more confectioners' sugar if it is too thin.

3. Use a paintbrush to spread cookie paint evenly onto the cookie. Place each finished cookie on the cooling rack or a serving plate to dry. Make more cookie paint if necessary. To make extra-creamy cookie paint, use two teaspoons of water when mixing.

Building Things

Wooden Tool Box

Bottle Cap Name Plaque

Coffee Can Bird Feeder

Paper Sailboat

Cardboard Box Playhouse

Shoebox Dollhouse

Berry Box Doll Furniture

Clothespin People

Wooden Tool Box

Build a wooden box for storing your tools in a handy way. Ask an adult to help you cut the wood and set up materials for your project.

MATERIALS NEEDED

Pencil

Ruler or measuring stick

Tracing paper

Scrap wood,
about $\frac{1}{2}$ to $\frac{3}{4}$-inch thick

Handsaw

Hammer

Finishing nails,
($1\frac{1}{2}$ inch or size 4d)

1. Assemble materials on your work surface.

2. **End Panels (A):** Trace the red dotted shape *(page 113)* on a piece of tracing paper. Cut shape out. With adult help, use the shape as a pattern to cut out two end panels.

Bottom (B): With adult help, measure and cut one $7\frac{1}{2}$-by-12-inch piece of wood for the bottom of the box.

Front and Back Panels (C): With adult help, measure and cut two 4-by-12-inch pieces of wood for the front and back panels.

Top Handle (D): With adult help, measure and cut one 3-by12-inch piece of wood for the top handle.

3. To assemble: Nail the lower edge of A to one end of B (Figure 1). Repeat for the other side. You will have both ends and the bottom joined together.

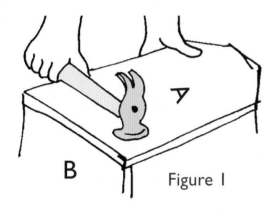

Figure 1

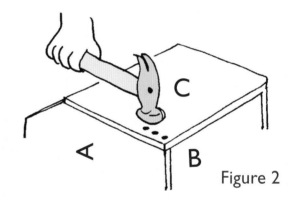

Figure 2

4. Next, nail the sides of C to the sides of A/B piece (Figure 2). Repeat the same steps for the other side.

5. For the last step, hammer the handle into place. Nail D to the top of A at both ends of the box (Figure 3). Now you are ready to paint your box and store tools in it!

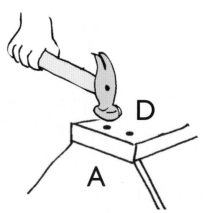

Figure 3

Bottle Cap Name Plaque

*This project is especially good practice for beginner hands.
Write your name, initials, or house number and hammer away!*

MATERIALS NEEDED

Newspaper, for work surface

Sandpaper

10-by-12-inch scrap wood,
½ to ¾-inch thick

Pencil

White glue

Hammer

Small nails or tacks with heads

Old paint brush

Metal bottle caps, assorted

Beads, dried lentils, dried corn, or dried peas

Strong string or rope

1. Assemble all materials on your work surface and spread out newspaper. Use sandpaper to create a smooth surface on the top and side edges of the wood. Use a pencil to draw your name onto the piece of wood. Draw it so the letters or house numbers are almost the same height as the board. (You can also make a decorative border around the edges with extra bottle caps.)

2. Use an old paintbrush to glue the front of the bottle cap and set it on the base of your first letter, upside down so the inside of cap faces up.

3. To hammer a nail, first pinch the nail between your index and thumb, carefully pointing the tip of the nail in the center of the bottle cap. (Be sure to pinch the nail underneath the head to protect your fingers when pounding.)

4. Gently tap the top of the nail head into the wood and pound until it is flat against the bottle cap. Continue until you have outlined the shape of your drawing.

5. Using an old paintbrush, brush a small amount of glue inside each bottle cap and fill with beads, corn, or peas. Allow to dry overnight.

6. To hang: Using your ruler, measure two inches in from the top edge on each side. Mark both points with your pencil. Pound a small nail in at each point. Tie the string around each nail and hang from a doorknob or a favorite hook.

Coffee Can Bird Feeder

Make a simple bird feeder fashioned from an empty coffee can.
Be sure to keep the bird feeder filled on a regular basis.

MATERIALS NEEDED

Newspaper, for work surface

Empty coffee can (washed, clean, and
dried with top end removed)

Snap-on plastic lid from coffee can

Bottle/can opener with triangular head

Hammer

Large nail

Twine, about 24 inches long

Craft knife or scissors

Strong tape

Whole, unhusked sunflower seeds

Outdoor housepaint, and permanent markers (optional)

1. Assemble all materials on your work surface and spread
out newspaper. Place the plastic lid over the top open end
of the coffee can. (This will be the top of your bird feeder.)

2. On the closed end of the can, punch openings along the bottom edge using a bottle/can opener with a triangular head. Press gently to make a series of small openings (Figure 1). Very carefully, push the inside metal piece back just enough for the seeds to come out slowly. (If you push in all the way the seeds will spill out!)

3. To make a hanger: Use a hammer and nail to punch two small holes on opposite sides of the top edge, just under the plastic lid. Remove lid and set aside. Working from the inside, string the twine through one of the holes and pull through about 3 inches. Again, working from the inside, string the second end of twine through the other hole. Tie together in a firm knot to form a hanger (Figure 2).

4. With adult help, decorate you bird feeder with leftover outdoor house paint and permanent markers. Let dry completely.

5. When dry, fill the can with sunflower seeds and place the lid on firmly. Use two pieces of strong tape to secure both sides of the plastic lid. (This helps to keep unwanted critters out.) Hang the bird feeder from a tall branch, away from the tree trunk. Within a few days your bird friends should begin to visit the feeder. Be sure to fill the can regularly as the birds will come to expect a meal from your bird feeder.

Figure 1

TIP *Keep a backyard journal of all the birds who gather at your feeder. Record their features such as colors, shape of wings, heads, as well as their feeding habits.*

Figure 2

Paper Sailboat

Make a fine waterproof sailing boat of folded newspaper coated with wax.
When using hot wax, ask an adult for help!

MATERIALS NEEDED

Newspaper, for work surface

Two 8½-by-11-inch sheets white paper
or newspaper

Candle (broken into several pieces)

Empty tin can, washed, clean and
dried, with top lid removed

Drinking straw, toothpick

Saucepan

Old teaspoon

1. Assemble all materials on your work surface and spread out newspaper. Take an 8½-by-11-inch sheet of paper and fold in half so the lower edge is even with the top edge (Figure 1). Crease the bottom fold with your fingertips. The folded edge will be down and the loose ends will be up (Figure 2).

2. Fold A down to the lower edge and crease well. Turn the paper over and fold B down to the lower edge, and crease well (Figure 3).

3. Unfold B (Figure 4) and fold back the lower corners (A) along the dotted line (Figure 4). Crease each side well.

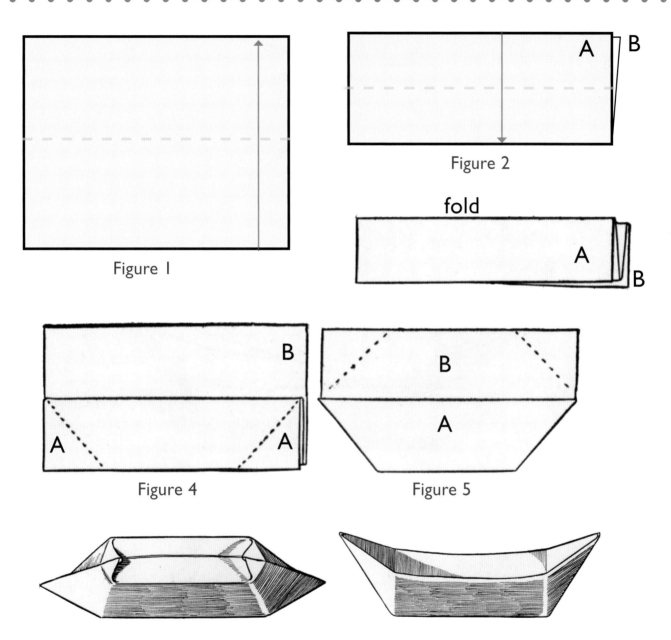

Figure 1

Figure 2

fold

Figure 4

Figure 5

4. Fold back the upper corners of B along the dotted line to meet the crease line. Next, fold down B to align with the lower edge (Figure 5). Crease well. (You should start to see the shape of the boat at this point.) Pinch in the outer edges to make the boat open. Set it upright on the table and adjust if necessary.

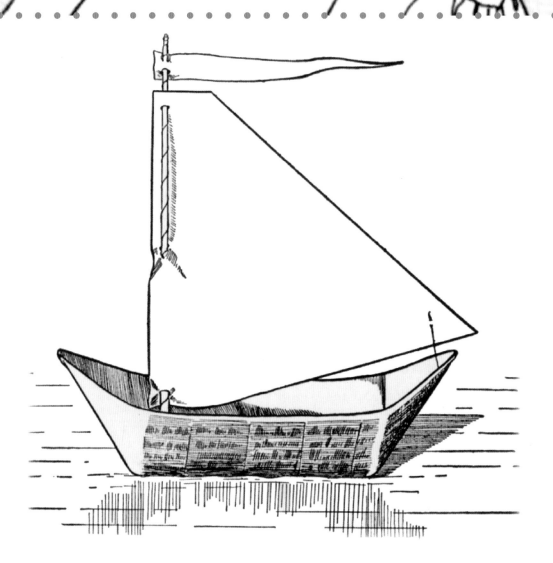

5. To waterproof the boat: Lay a thick pile of newspaper on the work surface. Turn the boat upside down on the newspaper. With adult help, place the candles in a clean, empty tin can. Fill a saucepan with 2 inches of water and set the can carefully in the saucepan. Place saucepan on stove over low heat and melt the wax slowly until it is fully melted.

6. Carefully dip the old teaspoon into the wax and pour it across the bottom surface of the paper boat. Continue until you have made a coating on the bottom surface. (Don't worry if the coating is a little uneven.) The wax will harden quickly so it is important to pour while the wax is still warm. Allow wax to dry.

7. To make a sail and mast: Cut a paper triangle out of an 8½-by-11-inch sheet of paper. It should be a little shorter than the height of your straw and no wider than the length of your boat. Using a sharp pencil or scissors, poke three holes into the paper, one in the middle, one close to the bottom, and one close to the top. Slip the drinking straw through the back and then weave through the other holes. Dab warm wax onto the front end of the boat and place the bottom of the straw firmly into the wax. Cut a pennant for the top of the mast and slip over straw or glue to a toothpick and insert into straw. Your boat is ready to sail!

Cardboard Box Playhouse

Make a playhouse for toys and stuffed animals that you can carry wherever you go. Your cat might even like to use it for a napping spot!

MATERIALS NEEDED

Large, rectangular shaped sturdy cardboard box

Craft knife

Pencil

Ruler

Masking tape

Markers, paints, colored pencils

1. Assemble all materials on your work surface. Find a rectangular-shaped cardboard box that has top flaps on all four sides. The box must have long sides and ends that are short. With adult help, use a craft knife to remove all the top flaps (Figure 1).

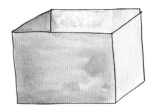

Figure 1

2. To make the roof: You need to score the long sides of the box to make the bend-in roof. From the top, measure two-thirds of the way down each side and mark each point with your pencil. Use ruler and pencil to draw a line to connect the two points (Figure 2). With adult help, use craft knife to lightly score across the line. Repeat for the other long side.

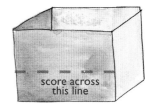

score across this line

Figure 2

3. Next, starting at the scored line, use craft knife to cut up along the side corner edges to the top. Bend in the long flaps so the edges meet to form the roof. Tape the roof together in one spot to hold in place (Figure 3).

4. To make the peaked sides: Use pencil to trace along both inside edges of the taped roof on side flaps. Use craft knife to cut along the lines. The peaked sides should align with the highest point of the roof (Figure 3).

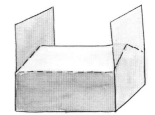

Figure 3

5. Use craft knife to cut two rectangular holes in the center of each roof to make handles (Figure 4). (Be sure to cut holes large enough for your hands to fit through when carrying.)

6. Decorate your new house. If your box is big enough, cut a doorway that your cat or other pets can fit through easily.

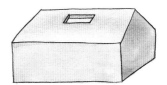

Figure 4

Shoebox Dollhouse

Make a small house for your favorite dolls using old shoeboxes.
Decorate it inside and out and design the rooms to be exactly to your liking.

MATERIALS NEEDED

Newspaper, for work surface

Four shoeboxes, same-sized

White glue or masking tape

Thin cardboard (for roof)

Ruler

Pencil

Scissors

Old paintbrush

Paints and markers

Old magazine pages, scrap paper, or fabric

Tape

1. Assemble all materials on your work surface and spread out newspaper. Set the first box on the table with the open side facing towards you. Use an old paintbrush to coat the top (or long side) of the box with an even layer of glue.

2. Place one long side of the second box on top of the glued box (the open side faces out in the same direction just like the first box). Press well and let dry completely.

3. Repeat as above for the second set of boxes. You will now have four same-sized rooms. Glue the short sides of your two sets of boxes together to make a four room house.

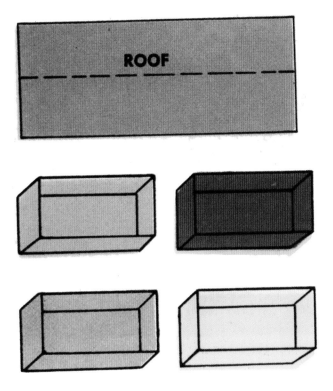

4. To make a roof, use a ruler to measure the width and the length of the house. Add an extra ½ inch to each end. Cut the cardboard according to your measurements. Draw a line down the middle lengthwise (as shown above) and use a craft knife to score or cut lightly along the line.

5. Fold the cardboard in half (along the cut line) to form a peaked roof. Place the roof on top of the long side of the shoebox and secure gently by pushing it down over the boxes. Glue or tape into place.

6. Using paints or markers, decorate your house with windows, painted walls, and window boxes. Wallpaper the inside walls with pictures from magazines, decorative paper, or draw small pictures to hang in your house. You can also make *Berry Box Doll Furniture (page 126)* or *Clothespin People (page 127)* to put in your new house. Use fabric scraps to make rugs and blankets.

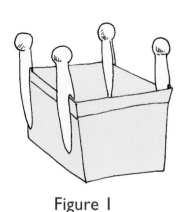

Berry Box Doll Furniture

Make your own doll furniture using only a berry box and wooden clothespins.
Use these simple materials to make a table and chair.

MATERIALS NEEDED

Newspaper, for work surface

1 one-quart wooden berry basket

6 round headed wooden clothespins

White glue

Index card

Scissors

Figure 1

Figure 2

1. Assemble all materials on your work surface and spread out newspaper.

2. Make a table: Turn the empty berry box open side up. Choose four clothespins and slide the prongs down over each corner of the box. Turn the berry box right side up so it rests on the clothspin "legs". Decorate your table with a small tablecloth cut from fabric.

3. Make a chair: Follow the same steps as above to make the table. Next, glue the heads of two clothespins to the back edge of each side of the box (Figure 3). Let dry completely.

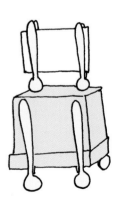

Figure 3

4. Make a back panel for the chair: Measure and cut an index card so that it is the width of the two clothespins you just glued. Glue the index card to the clothespins. Let dry completely.

Clothespin People

In no time at all, a simple clothespin can be turned into a doll or character .
Make a whole family of clothespin people!

MATERIALS NEEDED

Round-headed wooden clothespins

Markers and colored pencils

Scissors

Assorted paper and fabric scraps,
yarn and decorative trim

White glue

1. Assemble all materials on your work surface. For each doll use one clothespin. Draw eyes, a nose, a mouth, and shoes onto the clothespin using colored markers or pencils. Design your doll to look anyway you like.

2. To make an apron, cut a triangle of paper and trim off the tip. Glue to the front of the clothespin. Cut and glue yarn or string to the top of the clothespin make hair.

3. To make a dress, cut a rectangle out of paper or fabric scraps. Use scissors to cut fringes along the bottom of the fabric. Wrap the fabric or paper around the doll and glue the ends together in the back to make a skirt or dress. Tie a piece of yarn around the middle to use as a belt.

Toys, Games, and Pastimes

"Escargot" Hopscotch

Big Bubbles

Bubble Polo

Paper Cup Telephones

Silhouette Portrait

Shadow Pictures

Marbles

Clothespin Croquet

Jumping Rope

A Few Rules and Rhymes
for Jumping Rope

The Ferret Runs, How He Runs

Musical Water Glasses

"Escargot" Hopscotch

The word hopscotch means a short hop on a scratched line. French children play a version of hopscotch known as Escargot (snail) or "La Marelle Ronde" (round hopscotch). It is played on a spiral course and the players must hop on one foot to the center of the spiral and back out again.

MATERIALS NEEDED

Chalk, assorted colors

Sidewalk, good for jumping

1. With assorted colors of chalk, draw a spiral shape snail similar to the drawing on this page on the sidewalk— about six feet in diameter. Divide the spiral into fifteen boxes large enough for a foot to hop into. (They don't have to be perfectly shaped.)

2. Each player takes a turn hopping on one foot towards the center of the spiral and then back to the beginning square. The player may not step on a line or set the other foot down during her turn.

3. If the player successfully reaches the center of the spiral, she marks her initials in *any* square and calls it her "home". The player may use this square as a resting spot when taking another turn. The other players *must* hop over squares that are already "home" to other players. (This makes it a little harder to reach the center of the spiral.)

4. The game continues until all of the squares are marked with initials and no one can reach the center of the spiral. The person who earns the most "home" squares during the course of the game wins.

Big Bubbles

This bubble recipe makes big bubbles strong enough to blow across a table or floor.

MATERIALS NEEDED

Small mixing bowl

¼ cup liquid dishwashing detergent

½ cup cold water

4 to 5 drops of glycerin (available in pharmacies)

Plastic straw, 1 per player

1. Gather all materials and cover the table or floor with a thick layer of newspapers or an old tablecloth. Fill the bottom of the bowl with dish washing soap, cold water, and glycerin. Stir with the straw. Dip the base of the straw into the bubble mixture and carefully blow through the other end of the straw until a bubble starts to form. Continue blowing gently until it is the desired size.

Bubble Polo

This is a great game to play at a party. You can have as many players as you like.

MATERIALS NEEDED

Newspaper or old tablecloth

Bubbles and bubble wands

Four empty milk cartons, cleaned and dry.

1. Gather all materials and cover the table or floor with a thick layer of newspapers or an old tablecloth. Make goal posts at either end of the table using a pair of milk cartons.

2. The first player blows a bubble and gently sets it on the table. The player can blow three times to move the bubble to the other end of the table and through the goal posts. If the bubble floats off the table or bursts, then he loses and must wait for another turn. The game continues until the bubble mixture is gone. The person or team with the most points wins.

Paper Cup Telephones

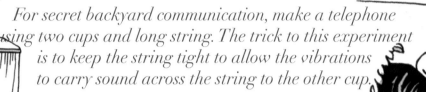

For secret backyard communication, make a telephone using two cups and long string. The trick to this experiment is to keep the string tight to allow the vibrations to carry sound across the string to the other cup.

MATERIALS NEEDED

Two large paper cups (clean and dry)

Large-eye needle

Nylon string, as long as you wish

Tape

1. Measure and cut string to a length that will stretch the desired distance. Use a large sewing needle to carefully poke a hole through the bottom center of each paper cup.

2. Tie a knot in one end of the string. Working from the inside of the first cup, push the string through the hole and pull through the outside hole of the other cup. Tie a knot in the end on the inside of the other cup. Place a small piece of tape over the top of each knot to secure.

3. Each person should take one end of the "telephone" and slowly walk away from the other person until the string is pulled tight between the two cups. The tautness of the string is what allows your voice, which is made up of sound waves, to travel through the string to the other cup. The vibration will transmit the sound. If the string is too loose, then the vibrations will not carry across the string.

4. Have one person speak into the open end of one of the cups, while the other person places the open end of the other cup against his ear. The "listener" should be able to hear sounds.

Silhouette Portrait

Make a shadow portrait of a friend using this classic technique for shadow casting.

MATERIALS NEEDED

Masking tape

White construction paper,
one sheet for each portrait

Lamp

Chair

Pencil

Scissor

Black construction paper,
one sheet for each portrait

Thin, white poster board

Glue stick

1. Tape a piece of white construction paper flat against the wall. Place a lamp on the floor. When you are ready to draw, turn on the light and remove the lampshade. Set the lampshade aside carefully.

2. Have your model sit between the light and the paper on the wall so that the shadow of the profile is cast onto the white paper. You may have to adjust the seating or the lighting to cast the proper shadow.

3. Carefully trace an outline of the shadow onto the paper—this is called a silhouette. When finished, remove the paper from the wall. Using scissors, cut out the silhouette, following the traced edges.

4. To make the final portrait, tape the white cut out silhouette onto black construction paper. Trace and cut out the shape. With glue stick, glue the black silhouette onto white poster board. Press well.

Shadow Pictures

Cast a light on a blank wall in a dark room, and, using your hands and imagination, create shadows that become magical characters. You can make shadow pictures of any animals you choose. Try making some of the shapes shown here and then try inventing some of your own.

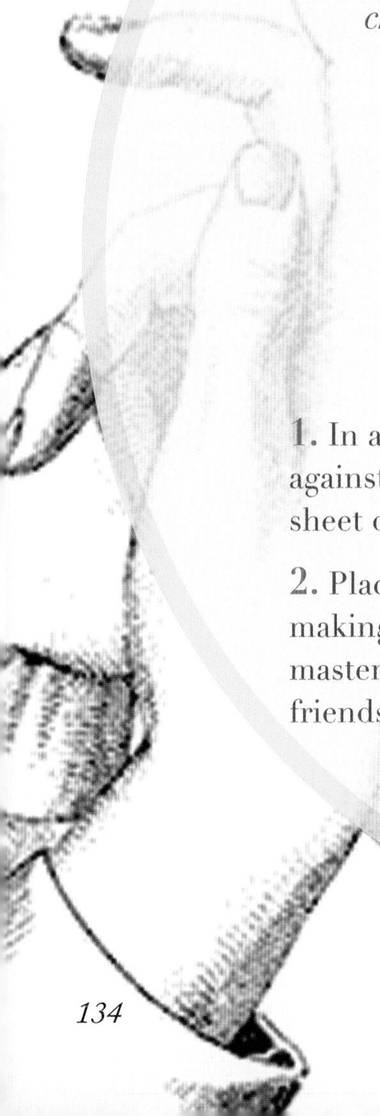

MATERIALS NEEDED

Flashlight

Empty wall space or white sheet

Imagination

1. In a dark room, set a flashlight on a table and beam the light against an empty wall to create a spotlight. You can also hang a white sheet over a bookshelf or on the back of a chair to create a screen.

2. Placing your hands between the light and the wall, practice making the shapes on this page using your hands. When you have mastered several characters, invent a story using your hands. Gather friends and family and put on a show.

Dog

Deer

Bird

Goat

Marbles

The basic game of marbles is simple to play. You only need marbles, a flat surface for rolling, and at least one friend (up to 6 people) to get the game started. Be sure to flip a coin to see who will go first.

MATERIALS NEEDED

For each player, thirteen marbles and one shooter

Chalk

1. For each player you will need thirteen marbles and one shooter marble. Shooters are larger marbles used to knock the smaller marbles out of the circle. Each player must have a different color shooter marble. The object of the game is to have your shooter knock the other person's marble from the circle.

2. On a sidewalk or flat surface, use chalk to draw a circle that is about eight to ten feet in diameter. Draw a 12 inch circle in the middle of the larger circle. Each player places thirteen marbles in the center of the smaller circle.

3. To begin the game, the first player kneels down at the outer edge of the larger circle and flicks the shooter towards a smaller marble in the center circle. The goal is to knock one or more of marbles out of the small circle without having the shooter marble leave the circle. The player collects each marble that he knocks out of the circle.

4. If successful, the player shoots again from the place where the shooter marble came to rest. If the player misses, or the shooter marble ends up outside the circle, then the player loses a turn. The next player takes a turn as described. The game continues until all of the original marbles have been knocked out. The player with the most marbles wins.

TIP: *In some versions, when the marbles knocked out of the circle are kept by the shooter. This is sometimes called playing "for keeps". To play "fair", all marbles are returned to the original players when the game is over.*

Clothespin Croquet

Real croquet is fun to play outdoors on a lawn. Create your own version of tabletop croquet using clothes pins and marbles for an indoor game. The rules are the same, except you roll the marbles instead of hitting them with a mallet.

MATERIALS NEEDED

Tabletop

Twenty clothespins

Marbles, assorted colors

Two or more players

1. Place two clothespins upright on their heads on either end of the table as your endpoints.

2. Join two clothespins together by sliding one into the other to form an arch. Set up nine clothespin arches or "wickets" around the table through which to roll the marbles.

3. Each player has a set of two marbles to roll through the wickets. The first player places his or her marble mid-way between the stake and the first wicket. Rolling a second marble, the player tries to hit his first marble through the wicket. The next player continues, each taking their turn. The first person who hits their marbles through all of the wickets and then hits the final endpoint wins the game.

Jumping Rope

Jumping rope may have originated in Ancient China and Egypt. It is said that ropemakers, while working, would drag ropes along the streets and children would jump in and out of them as a way to play and test their skills. Make your own jump rope and test your skills.

MATERIALS NEEDED

Cotton or nylon rope (used for clotheslines), about ten feet long

Scissors

1. To determine the correct length for a single jump rope, fold a 10 foot length of cotton or nylon rope in half to form a loop.

2. Stand with both feet in the center of the folded loop. Pull the loose ends of the rope up to the top of your shoulders. (The ends of your jump rope should not higher than your shoulders.) Cut off any excess rope above your shoulder height.

3. Hold the ends of the rope in each hand and set the bottom of the jump rope behind your feet. Raise your hands at the same time and swing the rope over your head. Jump over the rope as it comes down to the ground. Repeat. If your rope is too long, wrap the extra rope around the palms of each hand. Now you are ready to jump rope.

A Few Rules and Rhymes for Jumping Rope

Jumping single: One jumper uses a single rope. When jumping sing one of the rhymes below to help yourself keep the rhythm.

Bluebells, cockleshells
Eevy, ivy, over
Here comes the teacher with a big bad stick
Now it's time for arithmetic
One and one are two
Two and two are four
Four and four are eight

Mother mother I am ill
Send for the doctor
Over the hill
First comes the doctor
Then comes the nurse
Then comes the lady
With the alligator purse
Out went the lady
Out went the nurse
Out went the lady
With the alligator purse.

Jumping with three or more people: You need one long rope. Two people hold the rope ends and one person does the jumping. The jumper can invite another jumper in by singing the rhymes below. When the jump is over, the original jumper jumps out and the next person in line gets invited in by the jumper who remains in the game:

I like coffee, I like tea,

I like (name) to jump with me.

1 - 2 - 3 - 4 - 5

Jumping "Double Dutch": You need three or more people and two long ropes. The people holding the ropes are called "turners". The ropes are turned in opposite directions as one or more jumpers jump together at the same time.

The Ferret Runs, How He Runs

A traditional French children's singing game, you can play this game without a song and it is still very fun!

MATERIALS NEEDED

One length of rope, about 20 inches per child

One small ring

1. Take a rope and slip a small ring through one end. Tie both ends of the rope together in a knot.

2. The children form a circle with one child standing in the middle. Each child places their hands on the circle rope and passes the ring around the rope, making sure it is hidden under the hand. The child in the center tries to guess which person's hand is over the ring as it goes around. When he guesses correctly and touches the hand of the person hiding the ring, the game stops.

3. The child who was holding the ring is now "it" and goes to the center of the circle. The child in the center trades places and the game continues.

Musical Water Glasses

Make music with water and water glasses. Fill each glass with a different amount of water and try to make a song with a spoon.

MATERIALS NEEDED

Eight clear drinking glasses, same size and thickness

1 tablespoon for measuring

Food coloring, assorted colors

1 metal teaspoon

1. With adult help, gather 8 drinking glasses and arrange them in a row on a tabletop. Begin by filling the first glass with two tablespoons of water. Add four tablespoons of water to the next glass and continue adding the previous amount of water plus two tablespoons to each glass until all the glasses have been filled.

2. To test your scale, use a teaspoon to tap gently against the side of each glass. Adjust the sound of your musical scale by adding or decreasing the amount of water in each glass.

3. For extra fun, add a few drops of food coloring to each glass. Gather friends and give a musical performance!

INDEX

A

Acorn jewelry, 78
Animals
 cutouts, critter, 64
 envelope, 65
 shadow pictures, 134-135

B

Backstitch, 18, 38
Badge, owl, 79
Baking, 82-109
 basics of, 84-85
 biscuits, busy morning, 88-89
 bread, olive oil, 94
 equipment and ingredients, 84
 Irish soda bread, 86
 measuring ingredients, 85
 pie dough, double-crust, 95-96
 pie, peach, 97
 pinwheels, 98
 pizza, cheese, 90-91
 popovers, 87
 pretzels, baked, 92-93
 sugar cookie cut-outs, 106-107
 sunshine cake, 100-101
 tarts, little blueberry, 99
 terms, 85
Beaded cards, 54-55
Beads
 in acorn jewelry, 78
 in friendship pin, 75
 rolled paper, 70-71
 salt dough, 68-69
Berry box doll furniture, 126
Bird feeder, coffee can, 116-117
Birds
 blue bird ornament, 32-33
 owl badge, 79
 owl bookmark, 58-59
Biscuits, busy morning,
 88-89

Blanket stitch, 22, 27, 35, 44, 76
Blueberry tarts, little, 99
Bookmarks, simple, 58-59
Books
 folded picture book, 60-61
 little friendship book, 62-63
Bottle cap
 name plaque, 114-115
 pin, 74
Boxes
 berry box doll furniture, 126
 cardboard box playhouse,
  122-123
 sewing box, 10-11
 shoe box dollhouse, 124-125
 tool box, wooden, 112-113
Bracelets
 button, 72-73
 folded paper jewelry, 80-81
Breads
 biscuits, busy morning, 88-89
 Irish soda, 86
 olive oil, 94
 pizza, cheese, 90-91
 pretzels, baked, 92-93
Brooch, leaf, reversible, 76
Bubbles
 big, 131
 polo, 131
Building projects, 110-127
 bird feeder, coffee can, 116-117
 clothespin people, 127
 doll furniture, berry box, 126
 dollhouse, shoe box, 124-125
 name plaque, bottle cap, 114-115
 playhouse, cardboard box,
  122-123
 sailboat, paper, 118-121
 tool box, wooden, 112-113
Bunny, soft toy, 44-45
Buttercream frosting, mix-and-
 match, 102
Butterfly wind catchers, 52-53

Buttons
 bracelet, 72-73
 sewing on, 20

C

Cake
 sunshine, birthday 100-101
 cupcakes, fancy, 104
 decorations, cupcake, 104
 decorations, simple, 103
 frosting, mix-and-match, 102,
  104
Calendar, wall art, 56
Cardboard box playhouse,
 122-123
Cards
 beaded, 54-55
Chain stitch, 22, 29, 79
Cheese pizza, 90-91
Cloth, 12. See also Fabric
Clothespin
 croquet, 137
 people, 127
Coffee can bird feeder,
 116-117
Construction paper
 butterfly wind catchers, 52-53
 cutouts, critter, 64
 lantern, 50- 51
 silhouette portrait, 133
Cookie cutters, making, 107
Cookies
 colored sugar on, 108
 icing paint, cookie, 109
 sugar cookie cut-outs,
  106-107
Crisscross stitch, 22, 28
Croquet, clothespin, 137
Cupcakes
 birthday (variation),
  100-101
 fancy, 104
Cutouts, critter, 64

D
Doll furniture, berry box, 126
Dollhouse, shoe box, 124-125
Dolls, clothespin people, 127

E
Embroidery equipment, 11
Embroidery stitches, 22-30, 37, 52
  blanket stitch, 22, 27, 35, 44, 76
  chain stitch, 22, 29, 79
  crisscross stitch, 22, 28
  French knot, 22, 30, 40, 79
  satin stitch, 22, 26, 40
  stem stitch, 22, 25, 76, 79
  straight stitch flower, 22, 24
  up-and-down stitch, 22, 23, 76, 79
Envelope animals, 65
Envelopes, addressing, 55
Equipment
  baking, 84
  sewing, 11

F
Fabric
  raw edge, 12
  repurposed, 15
  right/wrong side, 12
  tearing, 12
Ferret runs, how he runs, the
  (game), 140
Flowers
  paper, 48
  straight stitch, 22, 24
French knot, 22, 30, 40, 79
Friendship book, little, 62-63
Frosting, mix-and-match, 102, 104

G
Games, 128-141
  big bubbles, 131
  bubble polo, 131
  croquet, clothespin, 137
  ferret runs, how he runs, the, 140
  hopscotch, "escargot", 130
  jumping rope, 138-139
  marbles, 136

musical water glasses, 141
  paper cup telephones, 132
  shadow pictures, 134-135
Garland, paper, 49

H
Hand sewing and
  embroidery, 9
Hemming, 19, 41
Hopscotch, "escargot", 130

I
Icing paint, cookie, 109
Irish soda bread, 86

J
Jewelry making, 66-81
  acorn jewelry, 78
  badge, owl, 79
  beads, rolled paper,
    70-71
  beads, salt dough,
    68 69
  bottle cap pin, 74
  bracelet, button, 72-73
  friendship pin, 75
  leaf brooch, reversible, 76
  paper, folded, 80-81
Journals
  backyard bird, 117
  leaf art, 77
  moon, 57
Jumping rope
  "double Dutch", 139
  making, 138
  rhymes, 139

K
Knots, French,
  22, 30, 40, 79
Knotting thread, 16

L
Lantern, paper, 50-51
Leaf art journal, 77
Leaf brooch, reversible, 76

M
Marbles, 136
Measuring baking ingredients, 85
Mobile, butterfly wind catcher,
  52-53
Moon journal, 57
Musical water glasses, 141

N
Name plaque, bottle cap, 114-115
Necklaces
  acorn jewelry, 78
  folded paper jewelry, 80-81
Needles, 11
  threading, 16
Newspaper
  beads, rolled paper, 70-71
  butterfly wind catchers, 52-53

O
Ornament, blue bird, pg 32-33
Olive oil bread, 94
Owl badge, 79
Owl bookmark, 58-59

P
Papercrafts, 46-65
  beaded cards, 54-55
  beads, rolled paper, 70-71
  book, folded picture book, 60-61
  book, little friendship book, 62-63
  bookmarks, simple, 58-59
  butterfly wind catchers, 52-53
  calendar, wall art, 56
  cardboard box playhouse, 122-123
  cutouts, critter, 64
  envelope animals, 65
  flowers, 48
  garland, 49
  jewelry, folded paper, 80-81
  lantern, 50-51
  moon journal, 57
  pastry bag, 103
  sailboat, paper, 118-121
  shoebox dollhouse, 124-125
  silhouette portrait, 133
  telephones, paper cup, 132

Parchment paper pastry bag, 103
Pastry bag, making, 103
Picture book, folded, 60-61
Pie
    peach pie, 97
    decorative edging, 96
    double-crust pie dough, 95-96
    Pie dough
    in blueberry tarts, little, 99
    double-crust, 95-96
    in pinwheels, 98
Pillow, toothfairy, 42-43
Pillowcase, embroidered, 37
Pin cushion, jelly jar lid, 31
Pins
    bottle cap, 74
    friendship, 75
    leaf brooch, reversible, 76
    in sewing projects, 11
Pinwheels, 98
Pizza, cheese, 90-91
Placemat roll-up pouch, 38-39
Plaque, bottle cap name, 114-115
Playhouse, cardboard box, 122-123
Popovers, 87
Pouch, placemat roll-up, 38-39
Pretzels, baked, 92-93
Puppet, washcloth, 40-41

R
Repurposed materials, in sewing
    projects, 13
Ribbon tie, 39
Running stitch, 17, 39, 40, 41, 43

S
Safety pins, 11
    friendship pin, 75
    leaf brooch, reversible, 76
    owl badge, 79
Sailboat, paper, 118-121
Salt dough
    beads, 68-69
    shapes and textures, 69

Satin stitch, 22, 26, 40
Scissors, in sewing projects,
    11, 15
Selvage, 12
Sewing
    on a button, 20
    equipment for, 11
    knotting thread, 16
    with repurposed materials, 13
    rules for, 15
    storing supplies, 10-11
    terms, 12
    threading needle, 16
Sewing box, 10-11
Sewing projects, 31-45
    bunny, soft toy, 44-45
    leaf brooch, reversible, 76
    ornament, blue bird, 32-33
    owl badge, 79
    pillow, toothfairy, 42-43
    pillowcase, embroidered, 37
    pin cushion, jelly jar lid, 31
    pouch, placemat roll-up,
    38-39
    puppet, washcloth, 40-41
    wallet, lunch money, 34-36
Sewing stitches. See also
Embroidery stitches
    backstitch, 18, 38
    hemming, 19, 41
    running stitch, 17, 39, 40,
    41, 43
Shadow pictures, 134-135
Shoe box dollhouse, 124-125
Silhouette portrait, 133
Stem stitch, 22, 25, 76, 79
Stitching. See Embroidery stitches;
Sunshine cake, 100-101
Sugar
    and cinnamon, 98
    colored, 108
Sugar cookie cut-outs,
    106-107

T
Tarts, little blueberry, 99
Telephones, paper cup, 132
Thimble, 11, 15
Thread
    cutting, 16
    knotting, 16
    selecting, 12
Threading needle, 16
Tissue paper
    flowers, 48
    garlands, 49
Tool box, wooden,
    112-113
Toothfairy pillow, 42-43
Toys. See also Games
    bunny, soft toy, 44-45
    clothespin people, 127
    doll furniture, berry box, 126
    dollhouse, shoe box,
    124-125
    playhouse, cardboard box,
    122-123
    puppet, washcloth, 40-41
    sailboat, paper, 118-121

U
Up-and-down stitch, 22, 23, 76, 79
Useful embroidery stitches, 22

W
Wallet, lunch money, 34-36
Warp and weft, 12
Washcloth puppet, 40 41
Water glasses, musical, 141
Wind catchers, butterfly,
    52-53
Writing activities.
    See also Journals
    envelopes, addressing, 55
    story writing, in folded
    picture book, 61